"Wow! If learning about business and entrepreneurship is best based on experience, Brian Cunningham hits a home run, sending the ball right out of the park with this book. *Never Give Up!* takes aspiring entrepreneurs right into the trenches to view the reality of creating and growing a business. A 'must read' for anyone who dreams of starting or running a business."

—*Nancy Nuell, Director of Business Development and Entrepreneurship, Montgomery College*

"Building a business is a journey into the unknown. You will not go down the same road as Brian, but his map described in *Never Give Up!* on how to reach your destination is without equal."

—*Dave Dicklich, CEO of ProjectorCentral.com*

"*Never Give Up!* is a great story that is very well-written. It brought back many fond memories of the lessons we learned along the way."

—*Bob Gibbs, former CFO of CES*

"*Never Give Up!* is both enjoyable and excellently done. Entrepreneurs and venture capital seekers will find this book a very useful guide to their success."

—*Gordon Macklin, first president of NASDQ*

"As a former associate of CES who enjoyed doubling his department's revenues as well as my earnings under Brian's tutelage, I can say that that working with Brian was the most enlightening aspect of my business career. Reading *Never Give Up!* helped me understand the source of his practical knowledge and filled in many of the big picture gaps in my own understanding."

—*Joe Newberger, small business consultant*

"Brian's account of the infectious excitement and day-to-day challenges confronted, as the company grew, is both graphic and compelling. A professionally rewarding experience for all fortunate enough to have been involved in the unique environment that only a start-up can provide."

—*Curt Mosby, former materials manager of Computer Entry Systems*

"After more than twenty-five years of working in the corporate world, I can state unequivocally that Brian Cunningham is the best boss for whom I have ever had the privilege of working. His style of managing by walking around and his sincere interest in each employee gave all of us the feeling that we played an integral part in the success of the organization. I highly recommend reading Mr. Cunningham's book, *Never Give Up!*, which will assist and empower entrepreneurs in building a healthy and thriving business."

—*Pat Sellers, former manager of administration of CES*

NEVER GIVE UP!

NEVER GIVE UP!

LIFE LESSONS OF A SUCCESSFUL ENTREPRENEUR

Brian T. Cunningham

Author of
Lessons for the Trail of Life and *A Workbook for Marriage Contemplation and Enrichment*

iUniverse, Inc.
New York Bloomington Shanghai

NEVER GIVE UP!
LIFE LESSONS OF A SUCCESSFUL ENTREPRENEUR

iUniverse books may be ordered through booksellers or by contacting:

iUniverse
1663 Liberty Drive
Bloomington, IN 47403
www.iuniverse.com
1-800-Authors (1-800-288-4677)

Because of the dynamic nature of the Internet, any Web addresses or links contained in this book may have changed since publication and may no longer be valid.

ISBN: 978-0-595-43221-9 (pbk)

ISBN: 978-0-595-87562-7 (ebk)

Printed in the United States of America

For permission, contact Brian Cunningham, 8616 Chateau Drive, Potomac, MD 20854.

On the cover: Mt. Everest. With an elevation of 29,035 ft, Mt. Everest is the highest mountain in the world. Brian Cunningham likens his entrepreneurial journey to climbing Mt. Everest for twenty years.

Permission to use and front cover photo by:
Lance Trumbull
Everest Peace Project
www.EverestPeaceProject.org

This book is dedicated to
Terri, Lynda, Johnny, and my kids and grandkids.

Contents

Acknowledgments

As with any undertaking, the end result is often due in large part to unsung heroes, that is, those people who lend support and encouragement behind the scenes. They never expect anything in return, but they are instrumental in ensuring ultimate success. A number of people have accepted that role in my life, and they deserve to be acknowledged:

My late wife, Lynda, the mother of our six children, accompanied me unfailingly on my entrepreneurial journey. Together, we struggled to simultaneously live the American Dream and raise our large family. From the founding of our company, Computer Entry Systems (CES), until its sale twenty years later, Lynda provided me with many constructive ideas and her unending support.

Johnny, my eldest stepson, energized me by saying, "You really ought to write a book on your corporate life. It would be interesting and helpful to people as they start or run their own businesses."

Terri, my always-inspiring wife, encouraged me to take Johnny's challenge. She has walked with me every step of the way in developing this book. And she never complained as she read and reread each chapter.

Jack McDonnell and Ed Etess, two amazing entrepreneurs who became my partners, started me on my own entrepreneurial journey. For that, I owe them my thanks. Thanks also go to our investors, board of directors, lawyers, accountants, and bankers. I couldn't have done it without you.

My associates at Electronic Sales Associates (ESA) and CES contributed significantly to my development and the companies' successes. They provided me with inspiration and opportunity to learn new lessons, and their efforts are largely the reason that our companies survived and thrived. These associates are too numerous to mention individually by name, but I thank and salute all of them for their contributions over the years.

Last, but certainly not least, my children and grandchildren never fail to encourage and stimulate me in my attempts to record what has been a wonderful and challenging life.

Brian Cunningham
October 2007

Preface

Entrepreneurship is a 24-7 job that requires commitment, attitude, planning, and persistence.

This book provides an autobiographical description of my entrepreneurial journey, including the good, bad, ugly, and humorous steps along my twenty-year journey through a valley of desperate despair to the thrill of corporate victory. I'm very proud of and grateful for the performance of CES Corporation, the subject of this book, as it grew from a few founders who had an idea to a thousand highly motivated associates on four continents. We competed, head-to-head, with the best of the best, including IBM, NCR, and Burroughs (now Unisys), companies thousands of times our size. And we won almost 60 percent of the competitive encounters. After four years of start-up losses, we achieved sixteen years of consecutively increasing profitability, returning more than thirty times their initial investment to our founding investors. While I personally made 98 percent of the mistakes an entrepreneur could make, I persisted, learned, and survived. Finally, CES thrived. I hope you enjoy this book as much as I enjoyed the journey.

In his groundbreaking book, *Job Creation in America*, David Birch reported that small businesses—those companies with fewer than twenty employees—were responsible for the creation of about 98 percent of all new jobs.[1]

Things haven't changed much in twenty years. According to the U.S. Small Business Administration, the above statistic hasn't changed at all.[2] For that reason alone, the message bears repeating: businesses with fewer than twenty employees are responsible for about 98 percent of all new jobs.

From an economic standpoint, America depends on the entrepreneur for the nation's continued fiscal growth. Certainly, starting a business isn't without challenges. Not the least of which is the failure rate. Estimates on the number of new businesses that close their doors within four years of opening run as high as 50 percent.[3] But such failure is ironically often a matter of simply not understanding how to succeed. On average, newly formed businesses require three to ten years of guidance from entrepreneurial veterans to substantially improve their survival rates.[4]

Unfortunately, not all seasoned entrepreneurs have the time or inclination to act as mentors for their young compatriots. I, however, have been inspired to chronicle my own experiences as an entrepreneur. I believe that my path may act as a catalyst and learning experience for those considering a similar journey.

My twenty-year entrepreneurial travels included a variety of successes and failures. I hope that after reading about my journey, budding entrepreneurs will learn to avoid the mistakes that I made. At least they may be better prepared to cope with them. They will then come to embrace and enjoy their own entrepreneurial journeys.

The failure rate of new entrepreneurial businesses doesn't have to be as high as it is. Although fear of failure can be a driving force toward success, if faced honestly and used to find solutions to problems, "never give up" is the single most important message I want to impart to readers.

I have written this book for three audiences: my family in order to provide them with a record of my entrepreneurial journey as they are beginning their own life's journey, entrepreneurs all the way from the most successful ones, that is, Bill Gates, Steve Jobs, et cetera, and my inner city-emerging victims of poverty, drug abuse, and incarceration whom I hope to help avoid some of the mistakes that I made as well as to give them tools to ease the burdens of their entrepreneurial journeys. It is for these reasons that I trust readers will find the appendices at the end of the book describing constructive dissension—a tool I found to be particularly helpful in stimulating my associates to achieve higher levels of intellectual performance. If readers use constructive dissension in conjunction with the questions at the end of each chapter, I am confident that you will get a great deal more out of your efforts to stimulate successful entrepreneurship.

Chapter One:

Climbing the Corporate Ladder

As entrepreneurs, we must have passion for what we are doing. It's up to each one of us to develop that passion!

Let me give it to you straight. I've had my fair share of first- and second-time failures in my many years as an entrepreneur. Over the past decades, I estimate I've made 98 percent of the mistakes that one can make in the entrepreneurial world. But what sets me apart from others who've made similar mistakes? And why have I enjoyed overall success? Despite the failures, and sometimes even because of them, I was resolute that I wouldn't give up.

Someone may have told you, "If you can survive, you can thrive."

That adage has always impressed me. I like the idea that if we persist and refuse to give up, we will succeed. Of course, the expectation of success must be reasonable. But what's reasonable? Who would have guessed that a couple kids with an idea for organizing the world's information on the Internet would find success with an innovative search engine called Google? Who would have guessed that a stay-at-home mom with a cookie recipe would eventually develop Mrs. Fields, a worldwide chain of baked goods stores? Essentially, it is most important to find your passion and then never, ever give up.

All human beings have a certain degree of intellectual ability. Because some of us have more innate ability than others, these endowed individuals would seem to have an advantage. Actually, in almost all instances, persistence levels the playing field. Having that persistence, that determination to never give up, allows you to analyze what went right and what went wrong in previous attempts. Determination propels you to try, try, and try again. It drives you to never give up. It may sound trite, but it's often true that slow and steady wins the race. The tortoise beat the hare not because he was a better runner but because he persisted.

I'd like to tell you that once I realized the importance of persistence, my journey was easy. But that's not the way it works. It isn't easy to keep striving in the face of adversity. It isn't easy to keep going when everything around you is falling apart. But I refused to give up. Because of that, I can now look back on my entrepreneurial journey and the bumps along the various roads I traveled and clearly say that it was all worth it.

Do I remember the exact point when I realized the importance of never giving up? No. But I do recall the point when I realized I needed to make a change in my financial life. Even though it occurred more than forty years ago, that day is still clear to me. I was only twenty-eight years old. It was July 8, 1964, just four days after Lynda, my wife of six years, gave birth to Karin, our fourth child. Lynda and I could not have been happier with our large family. In fact, we'd always thought that six would be a nice number of children. But on this day, I began to worry about our financial future.

As Lynda got some much-needed rest, I went downstairs to get a cup of coffee and to spend a few minutes alone with the newspaper before the older kids were ready to start their day. Almost immediately, I saw an article about projected typical college tuition costs over the next twenty years. Lynda and I had made a commitment to each other that when the time came, we would send our children to college. But as I sat there with my morning coffee, I realized the combination of the number of children we had and the projected college tuitions outlined in the paper meant that we didn't have a prayer of fulfilling that commitment, at least not on my current salary as a NASA physicist.

I had come to NASA when President Kennedy's challenge to land a man on the moon had inspired America. As a young physicist, I became passionately dedicated to meet the president's challenge. My job was stimulating and rewarding, but it wasn't enough. Regardless of any promotions I could reasonably expect to achieve while working for NASA, my job would never provide us with the kind of money we would need to send our growing brood to college.

I thought, "What are we going to do?"

To that end, I adhered to a basic principle that had served me well in the past. When faced with a particular challenge, consider all the facts. Then act, and do so immediately. Even though I wasn't entirely sure about the proper course of action, I clearly had to do something different from what I had been doing. I had to at least begin the process.

I considered joining the private sector because commercial engineering salaries were already higher than government salaries. I told anyone who would listen that I was in the market for a new job. I got some good referrals. Within a short period, I interviewed with Boeing, Hughes, Beckman Instruments, Hewlett-Packard, and others. Although there were many opportunities for me in the commercial world, I hadn't seen anything that aroused my passion. Past experience had taught me that I'd be much better off if I were passionate about my work. I knew that if I really loved my job, I'd outwork my fellow workers and perform well above average, thus gaining me the respect and the advancement I wanted for my family and myself.

Later in 1964, I was invited to attend an equipment sales seminar at NASA. A particular company was going to demonstrate products it hoped to sell to NASA engineers for use in the Space Race. As I sat in the exhibition hall that Friday afternoon, I listened intently as Jack McDonnell and Ed Etess, two persuasive Masters Degree engineers, turned salesmen, rattled off impressive equipment specifications and convincing application descriptions. The confidence, skill, and humor of these thirty-year-olds completely dazzled me. After the seminar, I approached Ed and Jack to thank them for their presentation. I didn't realize it then, but meeting these intriguing young men was my first step along my entrepreneurial journey.

I soon learned that Jack and Ed were developing ideas for an organization representing manufacturers. Their idea was to create a company that would market products for companies that could not manage or didn't want to manage their own sales forces. The men estimated that their company would earn a 5 to 15 percent commission.

I liked everything I saw in these two developing entrepreneurs. When they invited me out for a beer, I leaped at the opportunity, hoping I might gain a spot somewhere in their plans. Over several beers, Jack and Ed described their grand vision for the development of a representation company, which would evolve into a design/engineering/manufacturing/sales organization. After the sales company was running profitably, Jack and Ed wanted to create an organization that manufactured computer peripherals to ease the data input/output problems in the computer industry due to the ever-increasing speed of central processors.

Later, I eagerly told Lynda, "I hope I've found a place with Jack and Ed. It could provide us with an opportunity for wealth and success beyond our wildest dreams." I continued, "College for the kids is no longer a concern. If everything plays out as they said, money would no longer be an issue. All of us would have a chance to live the American Dream!"

I began to feel great!

Over the next four months, while continuing to work at NASA, I met many times with Jack and Ed. I learned more about how I might fit into their new organization, now officially named Electronic Sales Associates (ESA). Lynda and I spent hours discussing the pros and cons of my leaving the relative security of a NASA job, which offered somewhat limited, but consistent, salary increases, health benefits, vacation, educational perks, and above all, security for our family.

We wondered if it was a good idea for me to leave all that for a start-up organization when the two founders and I had a combined total of nine children and $10,000 in start-up capital.

In my case, I didn't have any real business or sales experience at a company more complicated than a lemonade stand. In fact, none of us had anywhere near the experience that we should have had to take on a venture of that size, but ignorance is bliss.

In terms of encouragement, Lynda, who was as intrigued by Jack and Ed as I was, said, "If we don't try it now, we never will."

I thank God that I married a brave and supportive wife.

In the spring of 1965, six months after we first met, I joined Jack and Ed as an account representative for ESA. Twenty-eight days after I started my new job, Ed asked if I could wait a week for my belated paycheck. This was my first introduction to Cash Flow Shortage 101. I began to wonder if our American Dream was going to be an American nightmare. Even though I was concerned, I shook it off and continued trying to sell our products.

Despite the initial cash flow problem, our timing could not have been better. The electronics and aerospace industries were booming. ESA expanded rapidly and successfully. Our first offices were in the basement of a beauty salon in Crofton, Maryland, a suburb of Washington DC. Within three years, we had offices in Washington, Baltimore, Philadelphia, and New York.

By 1968, I was an executive vice president of ESA with an equity stake in the business. We were then given the opportunity to take over the entire New England region for a number of the manufacturers we represented. While it was a fabulous opportunity for the company, taking on the new division meant that Ed, Jack, or I would have to move. I lost the flip of the coin and agreed to move my family, now up to five children, to Boston to organize and manage the New England division of ESA. Jack and Ed would stay in Washington and keep the cash rolling to fuel my start-up activities in New England.

We left Silver Spring, Maryland, and made the five-hundred-mile trip to Boston in a car packed with five children under the age of seven, our German shepherd, four goldfish, and any of our worldly goods that had not been squeezed into the moving van. I had a lot of time for reflection on that long drive. I thought about how well ESA had performed and how lucky I was to have the chance to do it all over again in New England. This time, I'd be essentially on my own. I also began to recognize the importance of timing in any decision.

ESA's founding was synchronous with America's race to the moon. This factor was more relevant to our success than our particular business acumen. If we had begun our business at an earlier or later date, we likely wouldn't have achieved the same level of success.

While timing may not be everything, it certainly is a large part of any entrepreneurial journey. As an entrepreneur, that's an important point to remember. Even if you are the best of the best, the timing has to be right. Else, you might as well stay home.

Chapter Two:

On the Road Again

A supportive family is an essential ingredient to becoming an entrepreneur.

We settled in the quaint village of Acton, one town past Concord. After overcoming the usual hurdles of finding a house, a school for the kids, stores, and a church to attend, my life returned to the typical cycle of spending sixty hours a week on the job and fifty hours asleep. The remaining hours were reserved for eating and leisure activities, including playing with the children, exercising, and hobbies.

At first, business in New England was tough. The former manufacturers' representatives had decimated customer relations. I could only obtain sales appointments by offering to right the wrongs of my predecessors. That taught me a valuable lesson. Once I openly admitted fault (even when it wasn't mine), apologized, and offered to fix the problem, customers came to respect me. Many even became my friends.

Within a year, the New England division was running smoothly. Shortly thereafter, it led the ESA pack in monthly sales production. Lynda, the children, and I came to love Boston and its people. We even learned to appreciate New England weather, primarily because of the winter sports activities that our whole family enjoyed.

Sometimes, too much success too early breeds discontent. A rift developed between Jack and Ed over ESA's immediate goals. Jack believed ESA was ready to move into corporate acquisition mode, but Ed thought the company was already overextended. He wanted to build a substantial bank account through sales before integrating other companies into ESA. It was clear to both Ed and Jack that, regardless of the company's next step, ESA needed a capital infusion to support any acquisition strategy and continue expansion. As such, Jack and Ed hired someone to solicit investments. Soon, due in large part to Jack's and Ed's past experience with Rensselaer Polytechnic and their sales success and gregarious personalities, we raised $140,000. For us, that was big money. When the money began to come in, one of our first actions was to hire Bob Gibbs, an old friend of mine from NASA, as our chief financial officer (CFO). He would provide a system of checks and balances for us, the wide-eyed entrepreneurs.

Over the next several months, Jack and Ed got into several arguments. Eventually, I'd throw myself into sales all week in New England and then fly to Washington on Friday afternoon to be the mediator between my two partners on the weekend. I had no idea how to go about mediation. I really was just winging it. Finally, Ed and Jack reached a compromise that, if I'd return to Washington to develop and manage a new ESA manufacturing subsidiary, which would meet Jack's desire to expand as well as Ed's need for controlled growth, they both would return to sales. In fact, they both excelled in this field.

As I flew back to Boston, I wondered how I'd present this new opportunity to Lynda. How would I tell her that we were to move back to Washington after only fifteen months in New England? I wondered if she would think that I was nuts.

I eventually decided that I was maybe crazy. I was being asked to take on the responsibility of creating a new subsidiary, a task I had no reason to believe I could handle. I had done a good job of managing a few salesmen and one technician for ESA in Boston, but the new job would require me to secure financing as well as recruit and motivate a staff of engineers, production people, salesmen, and administrators.

I thought, "Could I measure up to the task?"

After running a series of what-if scenarios, I was convinced that it was in the best interest of me, my family, and ESA to accept the opportunity. I gave my job in Boston to my second-in-command in New England and got back to Washington as soon as possible. I needed time to put together a plan for the new subsidiary that would design, manufacture, and distribute computer peripheral products. It was a bold undertaking. Once again, I was scared. But the fear of losing all we'd worked for with ESA exceeded my fear of starting the new subsidiary. Now, my biggest concern was how I'd explain all of this to Lynda.

By the time I got home, my enthusiasm for the new job had been reinvigorated. I was able to convince Lynda that our return to Washington was a good thing. For one thing, it meant that we could look for the country farm that we had always talked about owning. Together, we could raise kids, animals, and our new company all at the same time. We were sure we heard opportunity knocking again. Lynda then looked at me with a gleam in her eye.

"I have some exciting news, too," she said. "We're pregnant."

Our sixth child was born in February 1970. Six it would be. Our family was complete.

A couple weeks later, Ed called me with a minor problem. A number of our newly acquired investors had expressed concern because we hadn't been reporting on how their invested funds were being used. Their concern was valid, but truthfully, we had nothing to report. We'd been too busy settling ESA's organizational problems. In fact, we had burned through a fair amount of their cash just with operating and travel costs.

When one infuriated investor threatened to go to the Securities and Exchange Commission (SEC) about our failure to report on the usage of funds, Jack, Ed, Bob, and I decided that we'd better have a meeting with the entire investor group. We needed to reestablish their confidence.

I flew to Washington for the meeting. The purpose of my presence was to reassure everyone. My newly formed division had been advertised as the answer that ESA had been searching for and my job was to convince the investors that I was going to give them a return that was ten times their original investment. I was the new guy though, and I was beginning to panic.

"I don't know what the hell to say to them!" I told Ed and Jack.

Both brushed off my concern, saying, "You'll do just fine."

At that panicky moment, I realized my mission for the day. I had to help my audience identify with the problem on a personal level. Then I'd suggest a grand yet plausible solution to the problem, one that promised to put money in their pockets.

We were expecting fifteen investors for the meeting. Surprisingly, more than fifty arrived. We soon discovered that, because of the number of investors we had acquired through our previous solicitation, ESA had unwittingly made an inadvertent public offering of its stock, a violation of federal and state security laws. At that point, I didn't even know what it meant to be a public company, let alone an "inadvertent public company." I just knew that it sounded very bad.

We struggled through the meeting, but the investors were not appeased. Several threatened to go to the SEC to ask for an investigation of ESA, hoping that would allow them to recover their money.

Later, Bob called for immediate counsel with qualified securities lawyers, which led us to the offices of Hanson, Cobb, and O'Brien, a noted securities firm in Washington. During our meeting with Calvin Cobb, a tall, distinguished securities lawyer and former naval officer, we described the history of ESA and our current situation. Cobb listened attentively.

He told us, "Gentlemen, from a securities standpoint, your company looks like a car that hit a telephone pole going a hundred miles per hour. You only have one question to consider—do you want to go through the agony of trying to put the wreck back together, or do you just walk away and start over with a clean slate?"

Ed, Jack, Bob, and I looked at each other in disbelief. How could four well-intentioned engineers/salesmen/administrators have screwed their company up so badly in only three years? We wrestled with the ethics of our mistake. In the end, we unanimously decided that, if there was any way possible, we'd stay the course and make our investors and ourselves ultimately successful. We would work through the mess that we had created. If nothing else, we seemed to have found good lawyers.

I went back to Boston, packed up my family, and headed to my new job in Washington. I found us a rental home in Damascus, Maryland, where we could live temporarily. We called it the "Mills House," after the owner.

Situated at the end of a long, unpaved access road in the middle of a corn-field, the house didn't have any landscaping. The rental included a preg-nant horse and a crippled crow, which suited me just fine. We had wanted to raise livestock anyway. I thought this was a good way to get started. Lynda, however, wasn't as enthused as I was. In fact, she got tears in her eyes when she saw the home. It was so remote that our own six little "chick lings" wouldn't have any neighbor kids to play with. But good sport and good wife that she was, Lynda ultimately survived and thrived in this rural community, which was so different from her life on Woodhaven Boule-vard in Queens, New York.

So we began our life in Washington DC. I began my job as chief execu-tive officer (CEO) of the new subsidiary. Ultimately, Jack and Ed each went on to found their own successful public companies. Jack pursued transaction processing, and Ed thrived in air-pollution monitoring. I think it is quite remarkable that three people who met so serendipitously in 1965 could work so successfully together, at least for a period, and then individually go on to achieve their own American Dream of starting and successfully running public companies.

Chapter Three:

Failure Is an Opportunity in Disguise

If you can survive, you can thrive.

My years spent as a salesman for ESA served me well as I stepped into my new role as CEO. I had learned many things as I worked my way up the corporate ladder, not the least of which was the importance of never giving up. I learned that, if I could survive, I could thrive. Persistence would help me to get increasingly better at reaching my objective. But it wasn't always easy.

When I first began with ESA, I thought the best way to approach selling was to learn as much as I could about our products. My engineering-based logic told me that, if I knew the products inside and out, I could then bring this knowledge to potential customers and improve my chances for a successful sale. So I'd spend hours studying and memorizing all the facts about the products themselves as well as the many applications for which the products could be used. I then spent hours scheduling appointments, generally from contacts generated through "bingo cards," that is, cards inserted into magazines on which consumers checked off their particular interests and then returned the card to the magazine publisher.

On the scheduled appointment day, I'd arrive on time and look my best. I realize now that I'd verbally batter the unsuspecting customer, talking unceasingly for thirty minutes about the merits of our products. Then, hardly pausing, I'd spend another fifteen minutes expounding on all the other ESA products, regardless of whether the customer wanted to hear about them.

What was the result? I had limited sales success. Plus, I had many worn-out and bored potential customers who could not wait to escape my non-stop, energetic presentation. I was failing in my new career as a salesman … and failing often.

Insanity can be popularly defined as "doing the same thing over and over again and expecting a different result." Clearly, if I was going to succeed, something had to change. Both my salary and my family's well-being depended on it. Because I wasn't selling, I found myself in a catch-22 situation. I needed to spend money to make money, but I didn't have the money to spend. I finally decided to attend a local, well-known, expensive sales training school. Sometimes after repeated failure, it's necessary to reach out for a jump start to shed old habits.

In the second training session, my instructor suggested I begin my sales call by asking the customer, "Why am I here?" I was astonished because it seemed to be such an idiotic and impractical suggestion. I thought I was wasting my time and the little bit of our family's savings, on this sales training school. If I showed up for a sales meeting without knowing why I was there, any customer in his right mind would throw me out. At this point, the instructor redeemed himself.

He explained, "The single most important thing a salesman can do in a sales call is engage the customer as a full participant in the appointment."

So what could I accomplish by asking "Why am I here?" It was an illustration of how to get the customer engaged. Much to my relief, I began to understand why I had been failing so miserably and consistently with my sales technique. The instructors pointed out that the salesman's job was to attack the potential customer's specific problem as quickly as possible and then solve it.

I needed to ask my potential clients for the specifics of the problem that had encouraged them to fill out the bingo card. I'd then show them a solution to their problems through use of the equipment I was representing. To develop a long-term relationship, my priority had to be solving the customer's current problem. But I could not focus on this priority if I continued to talk nonstop instead of listening to the potential customer. It was crucial to get customers talking about their problems so I could affect a remedy.

Based on the lessons I learned, I completely modified my approach. From that day forward, I focused on talking just enough to get my potential client talking. I had to let them explain what was most important to them before I could attempt to solve their problem with the products I hoped to sell them. To keep this important sales process foremost in my mind, I developed a hypothetical sales assistant named CLARE:

- **C**oncentrate

- **L**isten

- **A**cknowledge

- **R**epeat

- **E**mpathize

The first four words ensure I have the problem clearly defined in my mind. The fifth assures customers that I understand their problems, both intellectually and emotionally. The result of my change was a much more vigorous customer interest in ESA's products. An unexpected benefit was that I fell into the habit of bringing new, and even more compelling, reasons why the customer should buy our products with each subsequent sales call. I was soon on the top rung of the sales quota ladder. More important, I was doing a much better job of providing financial security for my family.

Chapter Four:

Commitment

It is sometimes necessary to lose a battle in order to win the war.

In any successful entrepreneurial journey, commitment is one of the entrepreneur's most important allies. It should be your passion to be committed! Consider the following from W. H. Murray's *The Scottish Himalaya Expedition*:

> *Until one is committed, there is hesitancy, the chance to draw back, always ineffectiveness. Concerning all acts of initiative (and creation), there is one elementary truth, the ignorance of which kills countless ideas and splendid plans: that the moment one definitely commits oneself, the providence moves too. All sorts of things occur to help one that would never otherwise have occurred. A whole stream of events issues from the decision, raising in one's favor all manner of unforeseen incidents and meetings and material assistance, which no man could have dreamt would have come his way. I learned a deep respect for one of Goethe's couplets: Whatever you can do or dream you can do, begin it/Boldness has genius, power and magic in it.*

Murray's protagonist understood the importance of dreaming big and having the commitment to follow through on one's dream. It is a lesson I came to learn well in my years as an entrepreneur.

The new ESA subsidiary was to focus on products that could improve the data entry process, an innovation that was sorely needed. I first became aware of the computer input/output bottleneck when I worked at NASA. I often had to wait for hours for a keypunch machine to inscribe holes in a punch card. The holes represented alphanumeric characters. A high-speed reader would interpret the punch cards. The results would then be recorded on magnetic tape. Then, the information was placed on a disk, which would finally instruct the waiting IBM 360 computer to process thousands of calculations.

At NASA, such calculations enabled us to predict the orbital orientation of a satellite over ten- to twenty-year periods. Hence, they could predict the performance of our photovoltaic power supplies relative to the sun's rays which provided us with the information of how large an array we had to have and how to point it. This entire design process was expensive, time-consuming, and involved a large labor-intensive data entry process that required multiple people and machines, but it was the only way to enter information into a computer during the early days of the Space Race. At that time, I was only beginning to learn that every problem or inconvenience should be viewed as a potential opportunity. Now, armed with a strong commitment from my partners, a large and growing market, and an ability to attract innovative engineering talent, I was keenly aware of a potential opportunity and looking forward to the challenge to build a real company that Jack, Ed, and I still owned a large part of.

By the time I returned to Washington, Jack and Ed had contacted one of the principals that ESA represented with regard to data entry products. This particular company designed and manufactured IBM-compatible tape decks, the kind used to feed the disks that fed the computer described above. The company owner had agreed to design an inexpensive tape deck for an interim information storage system that, if it could be made to work cost-effectively, would negate the need for punch cards and the punch card reader. The information could be placed directly from the keyboard onto magnetic tape, thus eliminating one of the major bottlenecks.

By 1967, Mohawk Data Sciences, already a recognized public company, had successfully introduced a key-to-tape product, but it used the expensive replication of the same old high-speed magnetic tape for data storage. We believed that, through the use of our tape drive, which was much less expensive, coupled with real-time data entry software for validation routines, we could significantly reduce the labor and equipment costs for potential customers. We called this new device a "key-to-pooled-tape data entry accelerator." The key-to-tape idea wasn't mine, but I had accepted the responsibility for managing, financing, developing, and marketing it through my new division of ESA. I quickly realized that the key to my success would be a strong commitment to the idea. To reach that point, I had to believe in this product. Just as important, I had to believe that I could sell the product. I thus began what was to become a twenty-year entrepreneurial journey in the data entry industry with a complete reassessment of the potential of the key-to-tape concept.

In 1968, more than a half-million keypunch operators were operating in the United States. All of them were serving to convert typed, machine-prepared, or handwritten information by keying it into a keypunch, one keystroke at a time, to produce punch cards. I visited numerous keypunch companies in the area. The incredible speed of some of the operators amazed me. Some worked at ten thousand strokes an hour or 3.6 strokes a second. And yet it bothered me to recognize that the repetitive process of using one's eyeball and brain to digest the input character and then command one's finger to hit the correct translation key was a big waste of time for human beings. Intuitively, it seemed that there had to be a better way but until we had one there were over a million people (averaging two shifts/machine) looking for some degree of process improvement.

The challenge was intriguing. Becoming involved in the data entry field was a good idea. The market's growth potential was obvious and very attractive. My next step was to believe in the product that Ed and Jack had described to me in a way that I could accept for myself. I ran several calculations under best- and worst-case scenarios. I projected that we could produce a machine that would save customers at least 20 percent of their data entry dollars in terms of labor and equipment for the process. I concluded that a savings of 30 percent might even be possible if we could buy the parts and assemble the machines for the costs that I was projecting.

After performing these calculations over a period of weeks and then sleeping on the resulting projections I developed my own strong commitment to the key-to-tape product. I revisited the keypunch customers and found that a net savings, or increase in profits, greater than 15 percent would be sufficient for the companies to seriously consider upgrading their equipment. With this part of my assessment complete, I was convinced that Jack and Ed were right. There was a robust opportunity in relieving the input/output logjam. I gave a silent thanks to my partners for offering me the initial opportunity that now had developed into the new company and a new product. I was now firmly committed to doing all I could to make the data entry division a success for ESA.

But I wasn't entirely prepared for the next step.

Ed told me, "You're going to need to write a business plan to raise capital for the new venture."

I froze! I didn't even know what the term meant, let alone have any idea of how to write one. But my interest in and trepidation over this new assignment propelled me toward learning about business plans. At the library, I checked out all the information I could find on model business plans. I studied this material for several weeks. Finally, I thought I knew enough to put a plan together. I realized our plan would be presented to MBA graduates and other business-savvy professionals, so I knew it had to be as flawless as possible. It took more than two months of writing and rewriting before I compiled a decent enough proposal describing what we needed to do to become, within five years, a $50 million revenue, 10-percent-profit-per-year company. I also came to realize how easy it was to produce attractive financial projections on paper and how hard it was to make the plans become a reality. As the saying goes, "The devil is always in the doing."

Forty years after writing that first plan, I can look back and admit it was awful, but back then, I was sure I was ready for Wall Street, and I had read that Wall Street was where most entrepreneurs got started, so I decided to follow suit.

ESA didn't have any established banking relationships in Washington, so I looked in the New York Yellow Pages under "investment bankers" to find potential investors. Fortunately, almost every reputable investment banking firm has a division called "Venture Capital," which is staffed by the best of the business school graduates and experienced investment bankers. They listen to thousands of entrepreneurial dreams and pick the one or two that seem most interesting, practical, and potentially successful enough to warrant investment. To produce winning portfolios and take into account a reasonable number of losses, venture capitalists typically look for an average return of ten times their invested capital within five to ten years. That's a tall order, but the plan I had compiled showed that the data entry market was huge, needy, and growing so fast that it could support such a return. We needed $300,000 in early-stage financing to develop a prototype, test it, and prepare the rest of the company for our market debut.

I still remember that August morning in 1968 when Lynda made sure I was shined and polished. Then she kissed me good-bye and sent me off to breakfast with ESA colleagues. I planned to practice my opening lines for the Wall Street venture capitalists with them. I was so excited about my upcoming debut on Wall Street that I became a bit too demonstrative with my gestures, and I spilled coffee all over my new suit and tie. Fortunately, I was able to see the humor in it. After cleaning up the mess with some soda water, I was off to New York.

Getting first appointments with venture capitalists over the phone was relatively easy. They had not yet seen our business plan. For all they knew, I was describing a future Microsoft or Apple and yet these rare successes create are fuel that gave ESA the opportunity that we needed. When I began my actual presentations, I'd measure my success by how long my audience stayed with me before they ripped the plan apart, pointing out one flaw after another. Still, even their criticism was valuable. I'd make the appropriate corrections to the plan before my next appointment and then try again. Gradually, my business plan and its presentation took shape. I wasn't immediately successful on that first day in New York. But once again, I never gave up.

Finally, after two months and more than fifty rejections, I heard, "This is really quite interesting! Do you have time to describe the idea to my boss?"

"Of course!" I replied enthusiastically.

By that time, I could answer any questions with an ease that I could not have dreamed of having just two months earlier. Wall Street had done a great job of educating me, but for me it had been a very hard way to learn.

Around the same time that I started getting positive reactions to our business plan, ESA's attorney, Bob McLaughlin, called me to say that he wanted to introduce me to one of his lawyer friends. Bob and he had worked together at the SEC. His friend had moved to New York Securities, an investment firm in New York, where he worked with an investor named Jim Melcher, a successful stockbroker who was about to go out on his own as a venture capitalist through a new firm, First Venture Fund (FVF), that he was about to found. Jim had been very successful with his stock market selections in the late sixties, including making substantial gains for his clients in Mohawk Data Sciences, the data entry firm that I mentioned earlier.

In March 1969, eight months after I spilled coffee on my new suit, Jim wrote FVF's first investment check for $300,000, giving his fund 49 percent ownership of CES Corporation, ESA's newly formed subsidiary. Jim was so nervous as he wrote FVF's first check that he had to write it three times before it was inscribed clearly enough to be negotiable. Jim might have been a lot less nervous if he had been able to see twenty years into the future when he would receive more than a $10 million gain on FVF's first, and ultimately its most successful, investment.

Until that point in my business life, raising the initial capital for CES was the most difficult challenge I had faced. What eventually won the day for me was the physical, intellectual, and emotional commitment I made to myself in the process of developing our business plan. I concluded then (and still believe to this day) that, although the preparation of the business plan entails thinking through exhaustive details regarding the company's projected future, the most important aspect of the plan is the commitment and anticipatory what-if ideas that the entrepreneur and his team develop in the process of preparing the plan. CES wouldn't have succeeded without such a commitment.

Now that we had the money, we had to demonstrate that same level of commitment in executing our plan.

Chapter Five:

A Board for All Seasons

Every CEO deserves effective organizational balance.

After my partners and I decided to form CES to carry on the key-to-tape data entry development, I only knew one thing for sure. If I didn't raise money and do it quickly, my family would be in serious financial trouble. But I had no idea of the benefit that a properly organized board of directors could provide to a company. Now, almost forty years later and after having served in the roles of director, chairman, and CEO in multiple corporations, I have come to appreciate the tremendous benefit of a properly organized and well-run board.

In my early efforts to introduce CES and its product ideas to the Wall Street venture capitalists, I was surprised at how often I was asked who was on our board, where the board members came from, and what their particular interests were in CES. Clearly, no one was going to invest in CES without a qualified board of directors being in place. As I spoke with potential CES investors I gradually came to realize that from an investor's standpoint, the board provides a real- time, experienced, on-the-job check and balance on the company's management. The board is elected annually by the company's shareholders to represent them, including any venture capitalists who have taken a financial position in the company. I also began to comprehend that my intuitive business instincts could only gain from the successful experience of these business combat veterans. Once I understood the importance and necessity for a board, I compiled a list of notable people who I hoped to attract. Our willingness to form a qualified board was good enough to keep the due diligence process moving along toward an investment climax.

Admittedly, the financial needs of both CES and my family drove me. Consequently, my first attempts to build a board were specifically directed toward satisfying FVF's and Jim Melcher's needs. To that end, we decided that Jim would become a board member. Jim brought along Bob Uhline, one of FVF's founding investors, who at that time was the president of Schlitz Brewing. These two, plus Bob, Ed, and I, rounded out CES's founding board. Although our board members had good intentions, not all of them had the necessary business experience or appropriate qualifications for being on a board of directors. But, Jim Melcher thought the group was satisfactory, probably in part because FVF voted 49 percent of the stock. Additionally, Jim, with his outstanding mental agility and persuasiveness, believed he could persuade others to go along with his opinion when critical corporate decisions had to be made. If viewed from a larger perspective, however, CES's founding board fell a little short of a great board.

It was during this period that I also came to an understanding within myself that the combination of entrepreneurial zeal and the wisdom and experience of senior men and women willing to serve on a newly formed board of directors created the right blend of talent to significantly increase a new company's chances of success.

I was to learn later that writer and business advisor Peter F. Drucker (1909–2005), often considered the father of modern management, noted specific duties and responsibilities of a board of directors. If a potential board member can't meet at least one of these qualifications, he or she should not be recruited. The primary responsibilities of a board member are:

- Serve as operational check and balance of management's objectives

- Act as a conduit to affiliates who can assist the company in achieving its objectives

- Remove and replace any officer who isn't performing up to corporate expectations

While Drucker stated these requirements more concisely, over the years, I have developed my own ideas which I hope that readers will find helpful when choosing a board of directors:

Relevant Experience and Oversight Responsibility

If a board member is to be a significant contributor to the check-and-balance system of operations, he or she must have appropriate background experience within or as close to the company's industry, as possible. That is, don't take advice from someone who has no personal knowledge in the area for which he or she is advising. The same is true for oversight responsibility. If your board candidate hasn't previously experienced the responsibilities that he or she is being asked to assume, his or her questions during a meeting are not likely to be particularly relevant. Directors who have "been there" will gladly share their most harrowing business experiences, and this is what you really need, so be sure their experience is real and applicable to your company.

Director's Term

In building a board of directors, you are building a team of high-level corporate member specialties. It's virtually impossible to predict how the personalities of these executives will mesh. For that reason, just in case things are not working to the advantage of everyone involved, it is important to have a comfortable exit strategy through term limits. A two-year term usually works best, after which the shareholders can reappoint the director, or the director may choose to leave. This two-year approach also can serve as a source of corporate renewal by bringing new life to tired boards.

Special Duties

All board members should have appropriate experience and exhibit integrity, fairness, and prudence, but I think it's also helpful to ask each board member to take on a special duty that matches their strengths and avoids their weaknesses. For example, a member might give a five-to ten-minute verbal report at each board meeting on a specific area, that is, marketing, technology, finance, strategy, operations et cetera. This also gives each member a special forum in which he or she can demonstrate their special contributions to the company.

Remuneration

On my entrepreneurial journey, I have learned that, in for-profit corporations, proper incentives usually lead to superior performance.

Some people might say, "You get what you pay for." This saying also refers to your directors' or consultants' performances.

Smaller, newer companies are often initially unable to financially reward experienced board members to the degree that their backgrounds deserve. Yet, to achieve the success the start-up company desires, the company needs experienced talent at its earliest stages. To accommodate this dilemma, we developed a creative "engagement agreement" for board members and consultants. Essentially, a consultant or director declares his or her regular remuneration rate for the engagement, but he or she agrees to accept a ten-year warrant (option), priced at the current market value of the company, for his or her services. A multiplier (usually times two) is then applied to the director's or consultant's remuneration to take into account the time value and the risk associated with taking "paper" (warrants) in lieu of cash. Upon a mutually agreed event, that is, four quarters of consecutive profitability, the director or consultant has the right, but not the obligation, to sell his or her exercised shares or her vested warrant back to the company at the market price for which the company is valued at that time. This arrangement is beneficial for both the company and the director or consultant.

The Board as a Team

A potential board member may be quite successful in his or her own right, but that doesn't necessarily mean that he or she can play an effective role on your team. For example, as CES became more successful in the late seventies and into the eighties, we were inundated with opportunities to hire the very best talent in marketing, sales, engineering, finances, and administration from the most successful companies in our industry. Still, fewer than half of these well-intentioned, talented professionals could make the transition from their well-established, fully funded companies to an entrepreneurial company like CES. The newcomers, although experienced, were not accustomed to the lack of support services that usually exist in an entrepreneurial company and they were not able to succeed without them.

Eventually, we found a solution that was effective in building team play within a board. We brought board members together for a two-day retreat just after the company's internal retreat described in Chapter 12. We asked board members to critique the results of the retreat. As a result, within one month of beginning our corporate renewal, everyone, from the chairman of the board to the associates who delivered our finished products, was on the same page and catalyzed to move forward. It really does take a team to win in the corporate environment and the method described above worked well for us to develop teamwork.

Board Communications

One of the most important aspects of board communications is timely communication with its directors. My earlier experience with ESA taught me that it's absolutely essential to measure corporate performance at least every month. To fix a problem, you must know that it exists. Accordingly, at CES, we established the following corporate financial reporting policy that continued for the life of the company. The policy dictated that the monthly financial report for CES, including income statement, balance sheet, and cash flow, had to be produced within ten days of the close of the previous month. In addition, we developed a cover sheet depicting management's "early warning indicators" (EWIs), a set of facts peculiar to a company that helps them look into the future. EWIs go beyond the standard financial package. They signal that a company is moving in the right or wrong direction. Graphing these trends month over month and year over year will serve your company well.

Monthly reports, such as those cited, become timely and important information for your board members as well as for internal management.

In addition, if you have a policy of forwarding the monthly information to the board, you reap the side benefit of keeping your name in front of these busy people. A monthly report, integrated with quarterly in-person meetings, keeps the board fully informed. When a crisis arises, you can take full advantage of your board's wisdom and experience.

Another effective procedure that worked well for CES is to gather board members at a dinner the night before a board meeting. This gives everyone a chance to interact with each other in a social setting. Additionally, we often used this dinner meeting as an opportunity to describe what we thought the company needed to take away from the next day's meeting. Our executives and I always prepared the board members before the meeting for the issues on which they would be asked to vote. Board meetings are decision times. It's the company's job to provide the necessary collateral material in advance so members can make constructive decisions.

Chapter Six:

Creating the Necessary Alternatives

An entrepreneur must have alternative courses of action for achieving their objectives.

One of the most important lessons I learned on my journey was that an entrepreneur needs to have alternative courses of action in the likely event that the initial course becomes derailed. The development of alternatives for "just in case" conditions is one of the primary reasons for writing a business plan. It's an opportunity to consider as many what-if scenarios as possible during a time of relative calm. When the entrepreneur later encounters a difficult market, financial, or operational condition, you will have already thought through other ways of overcoming obstacles and achieving your objectives.

CES' key-to-tape product was developed to replace the 500,000 key-punches operating in the United States and relieve the logjam which exists between the availability of data and the high-speed processor. The speed of central processors continued to increase, which further exacerbated the problems of the much slower data entry process. We had made a strong business case to investors that our new product could provide at least a 20 percent savings in the combined data entry labor and equipment costs. At the same time, it could speed up the entire process. These projected savings were the foundation of our claim that we could build a profitable company that would reach $50 million in annual revenues within five years. We stressed the product need was great enough and that the market for a replacement keypunch product was large enough that our new company could secure a dominant position in this evolving marketplace.

We used the first $300,000 in funding to hire a small team of engineers, to outfit a facility and to build our initial prototypes. While our engineering team started work on designing and building the first models, my partners and I began looking for $1.4 million more capital. Our search seemed never-ending, but we needed the next round to initiate a limited production run and develop our marketing/sales team.

As CES's only salesman, I also committed myself to find beta test customers. A beta test is a post-design product field test in a customer facility that confirms the promise of new products. The selection of the beta test sites, as well as the personality of the site managers, is extremely important to the success of the project.

Great care should be taken in selecting beta test sites. They can directly impact the continued development of the product as well as the acquisition of additional investment and future orders. The general agreement usually states that the testing customer uses the equipment free of charge and maintains detailed performance records. In our case, the agreement also allowed for CES to bring potential customers/investors to the testing facility to see the product in operation. I was always amazed and gratified by the effect that the test site managers had on potential buyers as they proudly spoke about the increase in production using CES's new equipment. We also used these sites to demonstrate to investors that CES had achieved a viable product design and the opportunity to join in the investment was limited and quickly fading. If investors wanted to make ten times their investment, we advised them that they would need to invest without delay.

Meanwhile, Jim Melcher, our first and only investor up to that time, was in contact with me almost daily. He eagerly listened as I explained how FVF's investment was being put to work. His belief in his first venture capital project increased as the months went on. Jim was fully aware that CES would need a lot more money, and he was helping in the hunt.

One day, Jim called to tell me about one of FVF's investors, who was running a division of a Fortune 500 company, which I will call Company

X. While relatively rich in cash, Company X was coming off several years of otherwise weak operational performance. Although I wasn't yet mature enough to appreciate it, after almost one hundred years in business, Company X was in an early state of corporate decline. They were very much in need of a new and unique product for a large and fast-growing market. Company X already had a national and an international sales force as well as equipment service divisions in place, and they were looking for new products. It seemed to us, at least on paper, that uniting Company X and CES could be a marriage made in heaven.

Jim's investor friend directed Company X to send a team of engineers and marketing executives to evaluate CES's people, products, and future plans. After executing mutually protective confidentiality documents, CES engineers and I spent the better part of a year in numerous meetings, trying to convince Company X that our approach to data entry was the wave of the future. We also tried to convince Company X that to secure the market share that the product deserved, they would have to hire exceptional salespeople from the proven winners in the data entry marketplace, including IBM, NCR, Mohawk, and Burroughs. Regardless of how many meetings we held, we could not get Company X to close on a financing/equity/manufacturing/distribution agreement. Company X suffered from "paralysis by analysis," a condition I have seen many times since then, particularly in larger organizations.

Sometimes, Company X would send so many evaluators to CES that the group actually exceeded the number of people that CES employed. Meanwhile, time was marching on. We watched as new data entry technologies emerged that could threaten the potential large-scale success of CES's product. By this time, I was convinced that, if we wanted to close a deal with Company X in time to take advantage of the market opportunity, we needed to be creative and develop a plausible competitive alternative. After several seriously intense meetings, we decided we would introduce a "contract-signing stimulator," meaning that CES would initiate an action that it could control to stimulate Company X to close an agreement with CES.

Given this situation and the fact that the stock market was generally receptive to emerging technology stocks, we recognized that "timing" was on our side, and we chose to take advantage of it to raise alternative financing. Our board and attorneys counseled with us at length because the preparation of the SEC registration documents and the filing for an initial public offering (IPO) would be very expensive and time-consuming. And we were running out of both money and time at a fast rate. We finally agreed that it was worth the gamble. It appeared to be the only way to move Company X to an agreement. So, we introduced an immediate, legitimate, competitive threat that might deny Company X the opportunity of an exclusive worldwide marketing agreement to sell and service our unique key-to-tape data entry product.

Our lawyers and executives worked countless hours to produce the S-1 Registration Statement. If the SEC approved it, it would allow CES to sell its shares to the public. As soon as we got the first official-looking draft of our prospectus together, we made sure that the higher-ups at Company X saw a copy. It contained a description of the market opportunity as well as an immediate need for $1.7 million. At the time, when an IPO was held, it was common practice for the company's management to sell up to 25 percent of their own shares. That allowed for the difference in needed capital. The rest of the public's money, that is, the $1.4 million, was to be used to tool our product for mass production.

In all honesty, I didn't think we were ready to go public. From what I had heard, I didn't believe that CES had the management maturity to cope with everything involved in being a public company. Our timing was such, however, that, given the stock market environment for technology companies, we indeed could go public. It was a bluff, but it was a plausible one. And it worked! Thanks to the possibility of our IPO and the momentum we had built up with Company X's sales and service forces, Company X finally came to the table and bought $1.7 million worth of CES stock for 30 percent ownership in our company. This meant that CES was now valued in the aggregate at $5.7 million, which wasn't bad for a two-year-old company. Even more significantly, Company X placed an order with CES that was worth $20 million for the key-to-tape systems. They were to be delivered over the next five years. Additionally, there was a potential extension to double the order if the market took off. Our little company was off to a great start. I was sure all of us would be millionaires in just a few more years if the current pace continued. Jim Melcher was understandably delighted with his first investment.

Company X thought the only real risk was our possible inability to manufacture enough systems to meet the demand of their sales force. As such, Company X negotiated several onerous agreement provisions, including a provision that CES would have significant penalties for any late deliveries and would have to relinquish manufacturing rights to Company X if production quotas were not met.

On the day that we closed the contract, we were to receive a $1.7 million check as well as the $20 million system order at a ceremony to be held at Company X's headquarters. When I awoke that morning, I was both anxious and nervous—anxious to get my hands on the check and the order, but afraid that something would happen during the closing moments of the deal to upset what we had been working on for more than a year. We were so close! Finally, the deal was sealed. I was handed the check and the order. By that time the only thing on my mind was how I could get away before anyone decided the deal was all a big mistake and take the check and order away from us!

It was already late in the day when the last documents were signed. All of us were in a celebratory mood. After the traditional champagne toast, I explained to my new business partners that Lynda was nine months pregnant, and I felt I should get home as soon as possible. In response, they whisked me to the airport in a chauffeur-driven limousine with little flags flying on the front fenders. Wow! I felt like I had arrived! Once I was settled on the plane, a tremendous wave of relief washed through my body, which I sought to enhance with a Jack Daniel's on the rocks, my favorite stress-relieving tonic at that time. I fully intended to order a second one as I fingered the $1.7 million check and our $20 million order. This was the biggest check and the biggest order that I had ever landed and all in one day. Wow, was I happy! Then, almost as suddenly, I began to realize the stark reality of these two freshly minted documents. We had the long-awaited order and enough money to effect production. Now, CES had to perform. Fear began to replace my euphoria. By accepting the money and the order, we had agreed to finalize the design and build at least one thousand key-to-tape machines over the next five years. This was big stuff for a kid who didn't have much prior business experience, and I knew this was going to be a tremendous challenge for the company and me. I got off the plane completely sober. I wondered what would happen if we failed to meet the production schedule.

On the forty-minute drive home from the airport, I decided I needed to make this a night to remember for Lynda and our five children. I got home around midnight. Lynda was waiting up for me. We celebrated with champagne.

I suggested, "Why don't we wake the children so that each of them could hold the $1.7 million check?"

I thought it might be the only time in our lives that we would hold such a large check. So we woke each of the children. One by one, we tried to explain the significance of the check and the order for $20 million. We accomplished the first four presentations with the children with great fervor and enthusiasm.

However, by the time we got to our seven-year-old, Chris, who is now a broker/manager at Merrill Lynch, the same old story was wearing thin. Before we'd finished, Chris said he needed to go to the bathroom. To speed things along, I tried to hand him the check while he was standing in front of the toilet. Chris missed my handoff! The next thing I knew, the check was in the toilet. I scrambled to pull it out. In my haste, I crumpled the most valuable piece of paper I had ever held. But that wasn't the end of it. To my horror, I saw that the black ink of the authorizing signature was blurring right before my eyes. I ran to get a blotter, which managed to stop the fading. Then Lynda and I set up a makeshift clothesline in the kitchen and hung the check to dry. We went to bed that night thanking God for our good fortune and praying the check's soaking wouldn't prevent us from depositing it. I was imagining my embarrassment if I had to explain to CES's board of directors, investors, and associates that I had dropped the most valuable piece of paper that I had ever held, in the toilet.

The next morning, the check was dry. Lynda ironed out the wrinkles so it looked presentable enough for me to take to the bank. Fortunately, the bank wanted the money in our/their account as much as we wanted to deposit it. I told the bankers the entire story, and they processed the check expeditiously, laughing all the way. I look back on this event as my first and only attempt to "launder" money.

During those early entrepreneurial years, life had been exciting and challenging, but we had to be frugal. We only received pay when we sold something at ESA, and one of the economies that Lynda and I had employed was to limit frivolous family expenditures, for example, soft drinks. We only had room in the budget for soda pop on Friday nights. To fulfill this budgetary restriction, I used to make and bottle root beer. It was never very good, but it sure was cheap.

Our firstborn, Gail, who is now an ER Physician and Director of St. Joe's Hospital's emergency room in Towson, Maryland, asked, "Dad, does this mean that we can now have brand-name soda on Friday nights?"

Because our family's cut of the $1.7 million was $75,000, which was three times my annual salary at that time, I firmly answered Gail with one of my favorite action words, "Done!"

CES was finally properly financed for the task of building our company. Looking back, I had no idea just how much work lay ahead of me. If I had, I might not have stayed the course. But it's often true that ignorance is bliss, and so we forged ahead and eventually (ten years later) CES became a publicly traded company with one thousand associates on four continents.

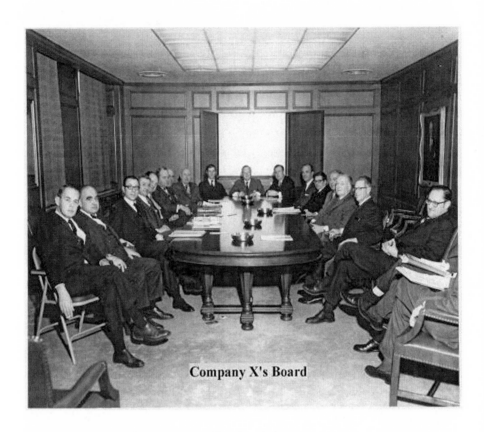

You can't tell a book by its cover!
Brian Cunningham (center right) and Company X's board of directors

President Y of Company X handing the author of *Never Give Up!* the check for $1.7 million

While I may look calm, what I'm thinking is, "How do I get away from this guy before he decides it's all a mistake?"

Companies that are asset-wealthy tend to fail slowly. In Company X's case, it actually took twenty-seven years before they declared bankruptcy. But the seeds of incompetence were clear in 1972, a full seven years before the final collapse began.

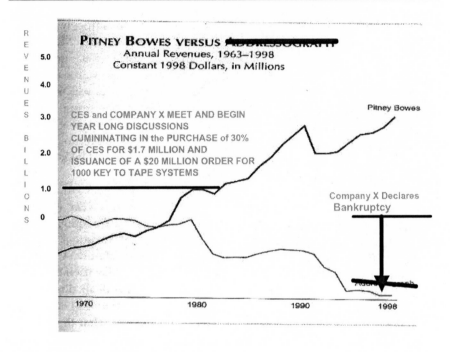

Although my associates and I were too immature to recognize "corporate decay," it was already abundantly present in Company X at the time that we executed our agreement. It took another twenty-seven years to deplete its assets, forcing it to declare bankruptcy while its archcompetitor Pitney Bowes grew. They were in the same industry, but different people with different management styles were running the companies.

Chapter Seven:

Persistence

Never, never ever give up.

The CES team was now feeling very good about itself. The engineering staff finally had the financial resources to complete the key-to-tape product design and properly prepare it for volume production. In addition, we already had a thousand-unit order to fill. CES would sell systems to Company X at $20,000 per machine at production rates that were scheduled to reach two units a day, adding up to $10 million in annual revenue all within the next two years.

Following the principle that a good entrepreneur should always have several alternatives in mind to achieve success, CES took a small portion of Company X's investment to initiate research and development (R&D) on an even newer and more exciting emerging data entry technology called optical character recognition (OCR), the automatic electronic reading of the numeric characters "0" through "9" and the alphabetical symbols "A" through "Z" in a variety of fonts or geometric configurations. If it were successfully implemented, OCR technology could eliminate most of the tedious key entry that our current products and those of most of our competitors were marketing at the time. OCR technology could also expedite the data entry flow and reduce data entry error rates. Our enthusiasm was quite high because of Company X's investment. We believed that, once we established a comfortable working relationship with this Fortune 500 giant, there would be a constant need to upgrade our product offerings to them. OCR systems would be just another product with which we would feed our newly acquired worldwide distribution/service force. The continuous flow of products would enable Company X and CES to fully capitalize on Company X's worldwide marketing, sales, and service organizations, thus producing substantial profits for both companies.

I thought, "Even though it had been a difficult year, we were lucky to have successfully developed this potentially great relationship."

At CES, we became completely focused on building our organization, including interviewing, recruiting, and training a first-class manufacturing and field service organization to teach Company X's worldwide service technicians how to repair key-to-tape machines. In addition, CES was responsible for assisting in the development of all the marketing, sales materials, and training and repair manuals for the new products.

Company X, however, was concerned because of the relative newness of our company and our ability to ramp up to meet their production requirements so that it could dominate the data entry equipment market. They felt that any failure to perform would undoubtedly be our fault because they had a track record of so many years of experience. My job was to prevent a CES manufacturing failure. To that end, we sought to recruit the very best administrators, manufacturing engineers, and trainers by offering them generous performance rewards for CES's corporate success, including ownership in our company through multiyear stock option grants.

For CES, timing was everything, and we once again found it working in our favor when we learned that Entron, a product supplier to the cable TV industry, which occupied the building adjacent to CES's corporate headquarters was about to close its doors. Why? Because the Federal Communications Commission (FCC) had put a freeze on the granting of new licenses to community antenna television (CATV) organizations. This action severely curtailed Entron's manufacturing business. In addition, Entron's management had exacerbated the problem by failing to diversify in time to save the company. As a result, Entron had to declare bankruptcy, close its doors, and sell all of its assets. At the same time, CES needed to find space and production equipment to fulfill the demanding production commitments that we had made to Company X. By moving aggressively over a one-month period, CES acquired the Entron lease, which gave us seven times the physical space we'd had previously. We also were able to inexpensively acquire a full complement of applicable electro/mechanical production machinery. Most importantly, CES acquired a superb manufacturing force, fully trained in materials acquisition, inventory control, sheet metal, and machine shop fabrication, electronics assembly, painting, quality control, and even shipping. The right timing and aggressive action enabled CES to take advantage of a wonderful opportunity. A nightmare for Entron was a boon to CES. We were able to build this tremendous team at a fraction of the cost we would have incurred if we had started from scratch. Opportunity had knocked and thanks to our timing in closing Company X we had both the cash and the need to take full advantage of this spectacular happening.

The news wasn't all good though. We had apparently made a major error in not requiring monthly sales performance reports from Company X. If CES had been able to analyze Company X's performance, it would have signaled the early warning signs, which are especially useful in analyzing a new sales effort with a new product, that the program wasn't meeting expectations. The reason for this was that during the negotiations, I had been afraid to demand sales projections or even indicators from Company X because I thought that my request would add another slow-down wrinkle to an already-too-slow-to-develop deal. I also believed that everyone involved, especially a company as experienced as Company X, would recognize the need to reinforce the sales force with relationship-based data entry sales professionals from IBM, NCR, Mohawk, and Burroughs. I was surprised and disappointed when there was no attempt to sweeten Company X's sales force with proven winners from the data entry market. Instead, for the first time in my life, I experienced the politics, bureaucracy, egos, inefficiencies, and jealousies of a large, well-established company turning sour. I can see now that Company X was in an early state of corporate decline and very much in need of what I later would refer to as "corporate renewal," a process by which an organization recognizes that periodic renewal must be proactively pursued in order to sustain a vigorous and prolonged life.

Over the following months, CES trained Company X's salesmen, field service representatives, and marketing personnel, but the irreplaceable, long-term customer relationships were missing. I was never able to convince Company X's management of the need to remedy this fatal flaw. As a seventy-five-year-old company with $500 million in revenue, it had become corporately insular and wouldn't listen to an "upstart" CEO with only two years in office.

Meanwhile, CES was required by contract to increase production to be paid for delivered equipment. We met those production schedules because we had committed to them, and we had to fulfill our part of the bargain. The consequences would be dire, for CES, if we failed. We increased our staff from twenty associates to one hundred eighty in just twelve months. I personally became involved with the hiring of most of these associates. I knew CES's existence and my tenure as CEO depended on our staff's ability to produce a quality product at a cost-effective price. We managed to acquire extremely capable people who were as interested as my fellow executives and I were in renovating the data entry market and sharing in CES's success.

Nonetheless, it was becoming increasingly clear that we were positioned much like passengers on the *Titanic*. We thought our "ship" was unsinkable, but it was now obvious that it was going down. I didn't know how or if we could save it. CES was meeting production schedules and receiving payment for the equipment, but the equipment was being stacked up in warehouses throughout the country because Company X wasn't selling it at the production rates stipulated in our contract. Company X's board of directors finally realized Company X had a serious management problem. In addition to CES's problem, Company X had many other crises in many other areas throughout the organization.

One day, Company X's board suddenly removed their CEO and replaced him with a former U.S. Air Force officer. Within a couple weeks of his arrival at Company X, the new CEO visited CES.

After a tour of the plant, where he saw robust production of his product, he announced, "We don't know what business we want to be in yet, but we're not going to spend another dime until we figure it out. You do whatever you need to do, but understand that we're not going to pay for another piece of equipment."

CES's problem was huge, and we didn't know how to respond to the new CEO of Company X in the light of our agreement. Cash is king, and whoever holds the cash has the power. We had one hundred eighty people working diligently and exclusively on producing the key-to-tape equipment for Company X at an operating expense of $300,000 a month. And based on Company X's statement, we had received our last penny of income from them. On the other hand, we had been able to accumulate more than $2 million in savings from previous shipments to Company X, which gave us the potential for seven months of life if we tried to continue at anywhere near the pace we were running at the day Company X's new president visited CES.

I immediately met with the key managers at CES to develop a disaster-recovery plan. We came up with alternative plans that represented different degrees of payroll reduction, pending discussions with our attorneys, Company X, and potential investors. I knew CES had a justified legal claim against Company X because we had fulfilled our side of the agreement. But none of us had anticipated that Company X would fail to meet its side of the agreement. Even if we took the legal route and sued them it would take months, if not years, to effect a settlement. Unfortunately, I had lacked the business experience to ensure that our agreement carried warning and repair procedures for Company X as well as CES. Company X's actions had caused CES as well as Company X itself to miss an incredible market opportunity within data entry.

In any case, all of our alternative plans shared one commonality. As a first step, I was to return to Wall Street to seek an investment that would enable us to create our own marketing, sales, and field service forces to replace those of Company X. I found several investors who were sympathetic to our situation. But after considering all of the facts, each concluded that CES had missed its window of opportunity to capture a viable share of the data entry market with its key-to-tape system. Therefore, we didn't warrant further investment. Investors just didn't believe that CES could sell equipment if Company X, with all its resources, had failed to do so.

In almost every case, potential investors asked a similar question, "Because you are losing money at the rate of $300,000 a month, what are you going to do if you can't raise any new money?"

In answer, I described our various alternative plans, but I always finished with the proclamation that CES would survive. This was a brave, but somewhat incredible statement, given the situation at that time. But it was during this tenuous period that I adopted the maxim, "If you can survive, you will thrive."

CES was running out of money very quickly. Settlement negotiations with Company X were moving very slowly. After management deliberations, CES management reluctantly decided that we needed to lay off one hundred forty people, or 75 percent of its workforce, in order to give the company a shot at survival. On the day before our layoff, I felt that I needed one final sanity check, and so I audaciously contacted Peter F. Drucker, whom many authorities considered the foremost business consultant of our time. He was kind enough to take my call, hear me out, and offer advice. I will be eternally grateful for his generosity and compassion. His sage advice meant the world to me. He told me that there was nothing else to do except "cut and cut deeply."

I met once again with CES's senior management to apprise them of my conversation with Dr. Drucker. I then sadly announced we would have to immediately lay off most of our associates. This move essentially erased most of the team that CES had spent the previous three years building. It was then and remains the hardest day of my business career, and I still believe even forty years later that it all could have been avoided if the management at Company X had been more willing to listen and act intelligently.

One of the best things we did as part of the layoff was keep our director of human resources for an additional ninety days for the sole purpose of assisting those associates who had been laid off to get new employment. She helped them in their search for new jobs, researching and calling likely employers as well as writing letters of recommendation, explaining the reasons for our layoff. This consideration, combined with CES's caring personnel policies, paid unexpected, but handsome, dividends when CES later emerged as an industry leader in the field of OCR and many of our former associates knocked on our door to rejoin us. And, this was at a time when the American economy was booming and the unemployment rate was extremely low.

Getting myself out of bed on the day after the layoff was very difficult. However, with a family as well as a company to run, I had to make a strong showing on both fronts. So I steeled myself as I walked into the cavernous building in which, just the day before, almost five times as many people had bustled about producing key-to-tape data entry equipment. Senior management gathered in our now-oversized conference room. We reassessed the data entry market and how it had evolved. We knew that it wasn't beyond our reach. During our three-year dance with Company X, competitors had emerged. The advances that these competitors achieved made our original premise of gaining and holding a dominant market share impossible, at least as far as the key-to-tape market was concerned. To dominate the market, we needed a large, well-oiled sales/service force, such as we had hoped Company X would provide. Now we were back to the beginning.

After much discussion, including threats of lawsuits, we settled with Company X for the return of the $1.7 million in CES stock they owned and a cash amount of $800,000. CES used the cash to pay down its many creditors. Our relationship with Company X was over, but we had our company back. Additionally, we had enough cash, if we managed it carefully, to make a new beginning. Most importantly, we had learned lessons that would serve us well in the future.

In retrospect, and even after forty years of thinking about CES's force reduction day, I cringe because of all of the damage I caused to so many loyal, hardworking, and gifted associates who had joined us along with their families to make a difference in the data entry field. It was my worst day ever, in business.

CES decided to stay in the data entry field because it was a vast and growing market. There were still potential opportunities. We felt we had gained significant knowledge through our aborted experience with Company X. We knew we had to look well beyond the key-to-tape products because key-to-disk systems were already replacing them. For us, key-to-tape had been a failure. Essentially, we had failed to take advantage of a tremendous opportunity by not requiring a more organized and specific performance agreement from Company X. After considerable deliberation, we decided to use the funds CES had left to shoot for the stars. We would leapfrog right over the key-entry systems and go for the newer and potentially much better OCR technology. If successful, the OCR technology would substantially reduce the need for the laborious and error-prone key-entry process. Once again, CES had an opportunity to reap significant financial rewards. But we did have a long way to go! The key to it all, however, was our common mantra: "Never, never ever give up!"

Several years later, when we had survived and I returned to Wall Street to seek another round of financing for our newer OCR systems, my earlier statement that CES would survive paid an unexpected dividend. I easily got appointments with senior investment people because they could not believe that we had, in fact, survived. Venture capitalists understand that a large percentage of their investments will fail, but CES had survived. They wanted to know the intimate details of how we accomplished it and in so doing gave us the opportunity for another round of financing.

Chapter Eight:

Shooting for the Stars

The devil is always in the doing.

OCR was, and is, potentially one of the most attractive methods for computer data entry. The technology had been around since the late fifties, but the complexity of its inherent multiple disciplines had thus far precluded its large-scale industrial adoption. Farrington Business Machines, a pioneer in the OCR field, had delivered the first commercially available system to Bank of America in 1957. Even today, OCR still is the ideal system for data entry. When correctly implemented, OCR can automatically scan machine-printed documents at high speeds with an electronic eye and read the preprinted information with greater accuracy and significantly reduced labor costs, when compared to laborious key data entry. IBM, NCR, Burroughs, and many other lesser-known companies saw the enormous benefits of OCR and committed tens of millions of dollars to the development of products to read machine- and hand-printed characters in many languages on a variety of paper weights and sizes. However, in order to justify purchasing OCR machines, manufacturers had to process increasingly higher volumes of data. This created a new set of problems because the machines ran so fast that they constantly broke down and frequently jammed, which significantly reduced their advertised efficiencies.

Given CES's state of corporate depression, both emotionally and intellectually, as well as the competition in the OCR industry at the time of our layoff, we realized that revitalizing our project in OCR was difficult and risky. We would need to develop something truly significant so that we could overcome the black mark that our recent product failure had left on CES. Fortunately, our product planners discovered a useful application known as Remittance Processing (RP). The RP application accounted for tens of millions of transactions each day and happens whenever a scannable bill was paid. The objective of the RP system is to facilitate the capture of financial account information so that banks can record maximum interest at the lowest labor and equipment cost. The more we talked about the application, the more excited we became about the possibility of using our lower-cost, potentially more reliable reading technology to develop a unique market winner.

Reading accuracy can be a serious problem for OCR devices, especially in terms of the substitution rate, which occurs when the machine reads, for example, a 2 for a 5, or a 3 for an 8. A misread might mean that the machine would debit an account of $8 million instead of $3 million or credit a client with $5 million rather than $2 million. The challenge for CES was to see if we could organize fast enough to develop a superior reading technology at a cost that would give our investors the financial return we had originally promised. All of us recognized that reading accuracy, including the all-important substitution rate, was the key to our market opportunity.

We reviewed our embryonic OCR development program, which we had started about eighteen months before the layoff. We foresaw the development of a niche market opportunity in payment processing (RP) data entry. We realized that our task was to develop a specialized, low-cost, reliable reading machine, complemented by key entry when required, to ensure the integrity of the input data. Our product would also need to reduce labor costs, improve accuracy, and speed the flow of information. Retail banks, insurance, utility and credit card companies, and municipalities would be the targets for our RP system. The possibilities seemed endless. Any company serving any industry that collected repetitive payments in large volumes was a potential customer for an RP product.

Focusing on the payment processing application would allow CES to limit the breadth of its reading requirements to the numerical characters of

0 through 9, plus a few special characters, in a limited number of font styles on a limited variety of paper stock. We were going to try to slice the available market into a CES-sized piece. It would be large enough to accommodate our growth objectives, but it would be within our abilities.

Because most of our competition had not considered RP applications, CES would sell reader components and transports as an Original Equipment Manufacturer (OEM) supplier to much larger companies, that is, those who had sales and service forces in place and were already trying to penetrate the RP market. It seemed a viable idea. CES management concluded that there were six reasons why we should take the gamble and "shoot for the stars":

1. CES's new product would be capable of winning in head-to-head reading contests, called "shoot-outs," using the client's test decks, that is, randomly selected documents that represent a valid statistical sample of the quality of material to be expected, which would demonstrate CES's superior reading performance. We allowed for all contingencies. For example, in the event of unreadable characters on mutilated or poorly printed vouchers, we designed our system to be operator-friendly so that intervention was readily and conveniently available. The broader lesson here is that entrepreneurs must create an easily demonstrated and important product differentiator(s) which are detrimental to the competition.

2. Thanks to the commitment that we had made eighteen months earlier, CES's OCR reading developments looked quite promising. It was mostly because of the superior technical leadership of John Guthrie, a technical visionary and our vice president of engineering. John had my full support, but I was hesitant initially. He was a brilliant engineer, but he had a reputation for being very difficult to manage. In fact, in our first meeting, John told me that his boss had been "an idiot who didn't deserve the air he was breathing." Nonetheless, if CES didn't have John's prowess, I'm sure that we wouldn't have enjoyed the degree of success that we did. I'm thankful that he and I learned to work together for the benefit of CES.

3. Developing and manufacturing OCR equipment required many of the same kinds of electromechanical manufacturing capabilities and personnel as the key-to-tape equipment. CES was already equipped with the capabilities and personnel because of the Entron bankruptcy.

4. Farrington Business Machines, just across the Potomac from CES, became overextended by making bigger and faster OCR machines. Farrington had to close its doors, making some of the best technical talent in the OCR industry available to us for the OCR development team.

5. Microchip manufacturers had made significant breakthroughs in device development in recent years, including reliability, miniaturization, and price reductions. These technologists created a chip called the "self-scanning diode array," which became the "eye and heart" of our newly designed OCR reader.

6. I was a proven and energetic salesman. I divided my time between preparing potential customers for our unique, highly accurate OCR reader and selling the excess manufacturing capacity at CES for an immediate cash flow. This strategy served to keep CES afloat while our engineers developed our superior OCR system for the RP marketplace.

Once again, our timing was crucial. We had very little control over many of these factors. When we recognized them, we were able to effectively and collectively capitalize on them.

Our financial wizards prepared a variety of business plans, including cash flows and income statements, allowing us to create balance sheets that showed that CES just might be able to pull off one of the great turnarounds of the decade with a lot of hard work and a bit of luck. Even though we faced the toughest corporate period of our lives, at least as compared to the disastrous day of CES's layoff, things were looking up.

As I left my office one evening, I reviewed the results of the past months. I realized I was fortunate. I had someone to love and something to do. Now, once again, I had a plan I believed in, and I could look forward to better days.

Over many years, I have learned the importance of these elements to a full and balanced life. I suggest you take proactive steps to make sure you have each of these assets, that is, someone to love, something to do, something to look forward to, and, most important, a plan to follow in your saddlebags for your journey.

Chapter Nine:

Finally, Breaking Even!

Always hope for the best, but plan for the worst.

From 1972 to 1974, CES and all of our associates were in a constant struggle for survival. On one hand, we had to hold off suppliers that we owed for merchandise that they, in good faith, had supplied us with to build the now-defunct key-to-tape systems. On the other hand, we had to scramble to raise money wherever we could to meet our payroll. To that end, we opened a data entry "job shop" to use the inventory that Company X left. This meant that CES provided production services, including labor, equipment, and management, to a variety of companies in order to more fully utilize its facility, equipment, and management talent. As we all pulled together just to stay alive, we reduced salaries and cut work hours as much as possible. We also adjusted our work schedule for full-time workers to nine hours per day on Monday through Thursday and a half-day on Friday, which everyone loved. In fact, long before flextime became so popular, CES offered this appreciated employee perk.

During this stressful time, I'd spend a few dollars on my woodworking hobby or buy a new gadget for the kids and me to fiddle with as we prepared our animals for upcoming 4-H competitions. From the close of work on Friday until Monday at eight o'clock, I always tried to devote the sixty hours to Lynda and the kids. In retrospect, given all of the circumstances at work, the time with them on our little farm was the healthiest distraction I could have had. It probably had a lot to do with saving CES and ultimately my sanity.

I also believe that CES was able to survive and thrive because we had the ability to cope with adversity, see the humor in sometimes awkward situations, and learn from all of our experiences. One particular incident demonstrates what it meant for all of us at CES to experience a glimpse of corporate insanity, apparent unethical behavior, and ultimately the corporate integrity, understanding, and goodwill of one of the world's largest pharmaceutical firms.

After our layoff, CES had far too much space for its current operations. We decided to try to sublet as much as 75 percent of our building space. Soon after we began advertising the space, a professor from a local university visited us. He and his team had moved into the commercial phase of their biomedical development project, and as such they were no longer qualified for space at their university. We were offering a two-year lease at a reasonable rate, but we would not put up new privacy walls. We expected to reacquire the space at the end of the lease. The lack of walls meant that each organization would need to respect the other's needs, equipment, and privacy.

Even though the professor heard the attractive lease rate we quoted him and the duration of the lease, he clearly hadn't paid attention to the part about respecting each other's rights and needs. In the ensuing months, after regular work hours, he and his team freely used our fax machines, oscilloscopes, and telephones. We complained, both in memos and sit-down meetings. Gradually, our tenants began to comprehend what was expected of them. Meanwhile, it was becoming obvious to all of us that, whatever the professor and his team were doing, it was successful. They were getting a lot of attention from well-dressed business executives who looked, spoke, and acted as if they were from Wall Street. Over the first six months of his tenancy, the professor tripled his space usage, which helped with our cash flow, even as it left us competing for parking spaces with his growing company.

Things began to slowly improve for CES. We were meeting our frugal payroll and paying down enough of the debt that we owed to keep our creditors under control. We had not yet secured any confirmed wholesale orders for our OCR equipment, but the combination of the gross profits from the key-to-tape division, the job shops, the space rental, as well as the strict control of payroll and tightfisted management of expenses meant that CES was close to breaking even. OCR customers were warming to the extraordinary accuracy of our readers when we demonstrated them on their test decks. I was convinced that it was only a matter of time before we secured volume orders from customers as CES prepared itself to penetrate the payment-processing industry, which had by that time annual revenues of $100 million.

Technically speaking, John Guthrie and his engineering team were doing a great job. CES was developing incredible reading performance. I always asked potential customers to commit cash advances with their orders so CES could purchase raw materials. At that time, we were on a cash-and-carry basis with most of our vendors. I believed that, once the potential CES customers fully understood the accuracy of our reader, the competition would be eliminated. Thus, advances would be forthcoming and cash flow would, once again be positive. Things were looking up!

On a rainy Friday morning in 1974, the mystery of the professor's "doings" was solved. A smartly dressed young woman marched into my office and announced that her company, Pfizer Pharmaceuticals, had negotiated a multiyear lease with our building's owner, a Boston-based property-management firm. She informed me that CES had thirty days to vacate the building. I couldn't believe what I was hearing. Initially, I ranted and raved about the unfairness of the situation, but she just walked out of my office, leaving behind the thirty-day eviction notice. Feeling livid, for the first and only time in my life, I threw a chair against the wall. I threw it so hard that it broke through the wallboard.

Then I sat down at my desk and stared out the window. After all that CES had been through and with the progress we were showing, having this happen at this crucial point in time was beyond my comprehension. I thought fleetingly about jumping out of my office window. But I realized my office was only fifteen feet off the ground. I'd probably only sprain an ankle or fracture something.

Still, I felt completely lost. If we couldn't get Pfizer to retract their action, CES's life would be over. With the current state of our balance sheet and profit-and-loss statement, I knew we would have great difficulty in securing a new lease anywhere else. I decided to follow the advice I had often given to others.

I'd say, "When in doubt, seek a qualified constructive dissenter."

I'd seek someone who could help us work through the problem together. I called my longtime friend and attorney, Bob McLaughlin, who was fully aware of our recent corporate progress. He suggested I come to his office. There, we would try to sort out a legal remedy, if there was one, to the disastrous eviction notice.

Bob and one of his senior partners, Calvin Cobb, talked with Pfizer's attorneys and found that Pfizer and the professor were clearly within their legal rights. They had simply taken advantage of the fact that CES could not qualify for extended lease terms because of its precarious financial condition. Therefore, we were operating on a month-to-month lease. Understandably, any landlord would grab the opportunity to sign a long-term lease with one of the largest and most financially successful drug companies in the world. CES had no legal standing, but our lawyers and I discussed the ethics of what Pfizer and the professor had done. I acknowledged that CES had actually hurt itself by sharing the building with the professor and helping him with administrative and engineering tasks, which helped his product development and his image. Could this be an opportunity to get Pfizer's attention?

We drafted a letter to General Pratt, then chairman and CEO of Pfizer. In my experience, those at the top of corporations tend to be more compassionate and ethical than most of the middle- and lower-level employees. While not illegal, we felt Pfizer's actions were highly unethical. By that evening, thanks to Bob and Calvin, I had a two-page, powerfully worded summary of the chronology of the events, beginning with our leasing the space to the professor and ending with our eviction notice. The letter also suggested that, if the professor's project, a new type of computerized axial tomography (CT) scanner, was as successful as Pfizer had now publicly projected it to be, the CES building wouldn't be large enough to meet their production needs in any case. I requested a meeting with General Pratt within ten days. My goal would be to try to persuade him to change his mind, given the ethics of the situation, as well as the practicality of the size of our building versus what they had professed their needs to be. The ten-day delay was deliberate. During that time, we sent copies of the letter to members of Congress and many potential CES allies, as well as anyone else who might be able to influence Pfizer's management. I always carried several copies of the letter with me to show to anyone who would take a few minutes to listen to our story. In fact, one of the names in Bob McLaughlin's contact file was Bob Shafer, Pfizer's Washington public relations representative. Bob had known him for many years, and he also became a recipient of our letter.

Over the upcoming weekend, my Aunt Helen was scheduled to visit Washington to attend a New York Giants football game, in which she owned an interest. The night before the game, Lynda and I always met with Helen and a few of the players for dinner at the Key Bridge Marriott.

On this occasion, as after-dinner coffee arrived, Helen asked, "How are things going with that company of yours that I've been hearing about for years?"

After explaining the week's exhausting events, I handed Helen a copy of the letter to General Pratt. It was just in case she knew someone who might help CES. Helen took the letter. In the dimness of the restaurant light, she struggled intently to read it.

She said, "You're not going to believe what I'm going to tell you. In two days, I will be playing golf with the wife of a Pfizer director. What a coincidence."

Smiling, I replied, "Do whatever you can on our behalf."

To this day, I do not know how much Helen influenced the final outcome. However, four days after she played her round of golf, the husband of Helen's golf partner called to tell me that he had read our letter. He was sympathetic to our situation, and he would personally discuss the matter with General Pratt.

I will never know the degree to which these contacts impacted the final outcome of the Pfizer story, but I do know that they certainly didn't hurt our cause. In many instances, it isn't what you know but who you know that can make all the difference.

On the following Monday, two days after sending our letter to General Pratt, I went looking for new space for CES. I was still hoping for the best, but I was planning for the worst. I initially limited my search to a twenty-mile radius from our current facility. I found several places, including a brand-new building in Columbia, Maryland, just twelve miles from our existing facility. The space provided substantial opportunity for expansion. I took many pictures with the intent of trying to sell General Pratt on this site as an even more attractive opportunity … if and when I was able to meet with him. The new space I found would provide Pfizer with a more attractive long-term expansion alternative, which might result in CES being able to stay put.

As promised, I called General Pratt's office at the end of the week. I talked to his administrative aide, who dutifully but with unusual attentiveness advised me that General Pratt was unavailable, but that an arrangement had been made for me to speak with the head of one of Pfizer's largest divisions. I was given an appointment in New York for the following Tuesday at 11:00 AM.

When the date and time arrived, I was in Pfizer's lobby looking my sharpest. I was escorted to my contacts office and after receiving an unusually warm greeting, given the circumstances of my visit, I described to the division head what had happened.

Then I asked, "What would you do if you were in my shoes?"

His answer was telling. He said, "I'd be so damn mad I'd want to blow up the place to …"

He then informed me of a series of mistakes and misunderstandings that Pfizer underlings had made with regard to the acquisition of the CES space. He said Pfizer wanted to make things right by transferring their attractive multiyear lease for the building to CES—if we wanted it. The eviction notice was withdrawn. Additionally, Pfizer would guarantee CES's lease payments for two years in satisfaction of the Boston property owner's request. Pfizer had worked this whole arrangement, and I didn't know a single thing about it.

I hardly knew what to say. In two weeks, a fatal blow for CES had been turned into an overwhelming victory. The problem wouldn't have been solved without the compassion and ethical maturity of Pfizer's senior management, whose behavior was a perfect example of owning up to one's mistakes, apologizing, and then fixing the problem.

Incidentally, Pfizer did move into the space we found in Columbia. As far as I know, they were quite happy there for many years.

About a month later, CES received its first large wholesale order from General Instruments Corporation (GIC) for one hundred OCR reader/ transports valued at $400,000, including an advance payment of $200,000. This order was the best news we'd had in a very long time. I personally went to GIC to finalize the deal.

Chapter Ten:

Have Check, Will Travel

Be creative!

Financially speaking, those five years prior to the order from GIC had been a rough time for all of us at CES. My personal relationship with various credit card companies had been pushed to the breaking point on several occasions. To reduce my stress and save a few dollars during CES's difficult years, I decided to personally overhaul my 1968 Mercedes 280S. The car was my pride and joy. Now, all I needed to complete the overhaul was a set of new tires.

I decided to drive my car to the GIC meeting. I planned to leave it at the local Michelin tire dealership to get the new tires mounted while I attended to the final negotiations at GIC. By 5:00 PM, I had the check for $200,000 in my pocket and the order for one hundred OCR reader/transports in hand.

By the time I returned to the Michelin dealer, I was exhilarated. My car had four brand-new Michelin tires mounted and balanced. I was ready to go. I couldn't wait to drive my car, and I immediately went to the office to pay my bill. I confidently handed my credit card to the cashier. I had used the last of my cash to pay for a cab ride from GIC. The credit card was the only means I had to pay for the tires. The cashier dutifully processed my card, but the authorization was denied. She looked at me quizzically, and my euphoria began to evaporate.

I knew I had been living close to the edge, but I thought I had enough left on my credit line to cover the tire purchase. Embarrassed, I asked for a phone so I could call the credit card company to try to persuade someone to authorize my tire purchase. After I was connected to customer service, I had to work my way through several layers of intermediaries before I finally reached a senior credit manager, who politely listened to my story.

"I wasn't notified of my delinquent status," I explained.

"Mr. Cunningham," he began patiently, "you are a businessman. You must know that my company is in business to make a profit, just the same as yours. We make a profit by extending credit to people like you. If everyone plays according to the rules, we charge our merchants enough to cover our expenses and have a little bit left over for profit. But I've just run a five-year analysis on your account. Our accumulated return on your card is minus seven percent. What would you do if you were me?"

I was surprised, impressed and depressed that the credit manager could so quickly quantify the negative value that our five-year association had brought to his company. The only honest answer was telling him not to extend me anymore credit, but I could not say that in front of people who had just mounted four expensive tires on my car.

Instead, I mumbled, "You should have advised me that I had used up my credit line, since I had been such a loyal customer."

That effectively ended the conversation as well as my chances of getting the credit card company to approve my transaction.

I then asked the Michelin desk clerk, "Can I speak with the manager?"

I felt relieved when he arrived in the attire of a mechanic. In my experience, people who work with their hands are easier to deal with than people in business suits. I explained my situation, emphasizing the significant trust that GIC had placed in CES and me. As I ended my tale, I pulled the $200,000 check from my briefcase.

I said, "GIC had enough faith in me to advance me this money." Smiling, I asked, "Would you, in the light of GIC's faith in me, be willing to accept my personal check for the tires?"

The manager hesitated a moment. I suspect he was wondering if he could trust this deadbeat who was overextended on his credit card. But then he looked at the check from GIC.

Nodding, he replied, "Yes, I would."

I was delighted. I thanked the manager profusely.

I said, "I'll call Michelin's corporate office and tell them how well I had been treated at your dealership."

I paid my bill and then drove home, completely happy in my beautiful, now fully restored Mercedes with a $200,000 advance in my pocket and a $400,000 order. Some days in the entrepreneurial world are better than others!

Sometimes, an entrepreneur needs to be able to think creatively, take a risk, and trust that people are willing to help.

Chapter Eleven:

Where Do We Go from Here?

Timing isn't everything, but it's almost everything. Take note of timing in your planning.

If the early and middle seventies were financial and operational nightmares for CES, the later half of the decade made up for all of the difficulties. We enjoyed a wonderful period of corporate growth and financial prosperity. In addition to GIC, our customer base expanded to include Bell & Howell, TRW, BancTec, CompuScan, Ameromatic, and Recognition Equipment, Inc., in the United States. We also had international customers such as Pixa in Germany and TK, a Japanese distributor that had been very successful in selling OCR in Asia. Our revenues soared to $8 million annually and continued to explode in successive years. By 1980, CES was back up to almost one hundred associates. I'm proud to say that many of those folks were returning veterans. They had been with us prior to our 1972 layoff. CES directors, investors, and associates could not have been happier. We also issued stock options to as many associates as we were allowed so they could enjoy the fruits of the team effort at CES.

The only dark aspect of this fantastic recovery and sales/profit growth was that the total available wholesale market opportunity for OCR reader/transports was only about $12 million annually, and CES had already captured most of that market. We were a niche wholesale product supplier. Try as we might to sell to the bigger retail suppliers, including IBM, NCR, and Burroughs, they really were not potential customers for CES. The primary reason for this can be found in a factor called "not invented here" (NIH). In other words, even though our reading technology was dramatically superior to the technology of the large retail suppliers, these major companies maintained they had a reader "in development and almost ready for release" that would be far superior to CES's technology. This type of boasting is actually fairly common in industry. It's generally due to false pride, but it's also related to the fact that our competitors were spending so much money on R&D that they truly believed that it couldn't be long before they would surpass our technology. While CES wasn't able to sell to the large companies, we took great pride in the fact that none of these giants was ever able to exceed our product's superior reading performance.

Still CES had a problem, because the large companies were not potential customers and CES had captured almost all of its potential market by 1980. Therefore, we had limited upside growth potential going forward. We concluded we could only continue to grow in sales and profits if we moved into a new field or acquired a greater share of the OCR data entry markets through one of two processes: forward integration or backward integration.

• **Forward integration:** We could broaden our product line and compete with our wholesale customers by going directly into the retail market. In effect, this meant that CES would be competing with the very same customers to which our wholesale products were distributed.

• **Backward integration:** We would get into the semiconductor manufacturing market and produce the microchips that we used in our reader/transports.

None of us believed that CES had the technology, financial resources, or marketing experience to engage in backward integration. We were in a catch-22! Each of these courses was fraught with significant risks. Either we needed to enter an area of technology that was unknown to CES, or enter into direct competition with the customers who had furnished us with our revenue and profits for the past five years.

I spent a lot of time writing detailed memorandums to myself on the pros and cons of competing with the very customers who had made us so successful. We studied the growth problem repeatedly. Finally, we concluded that, in the interest of the original intent of the company, our investors, management, and all of our associates, we had to take the risk and integrate forward. This was the most important decision that CES had made since the founding of the company. The consequences of the decision would determine our future growth—or lack thereof—over the next decade. If our forward integration was successful, CES would be positioned to grow to possibly $100 million in revenue. If we weren't able to make the leap, we could lose our company. Management made its recommendation to the board. After lengthy debate, our board of directors unanimously supported our proposal.

How was CES to move forward with this risky strategy, especially considering the changes that would be required to move from being a wholesale to a retail supplier? We decided to acquire our way into the market by offering to buy experienced distribution and service forces from current suppliers. Some were already our customers. We planned to differentiate ourselves through our superior reading and specialized magnetic inscription character recognition (MICR) printing technologies as well as forming important customer relationships.

We also had even newer technology advances being developed that we could bring to the market over the next few years to further our growth and differentiation. Due to our smaller size, our ability to focus, and the speed and quality of our engineering development team, we felt we had several distinct competitive advantages. The solution was to take CES public in an IPO, raise capital, liquefy our stock, and use the stock to acquire existing successful distribution forces. To do so, we would need board authorization to prepare and file an SEC registration statement and find an underwriter who would sell our shares to the general public.

Our IPO's success depended on our previous three years' financial performance as well as our investment banker's and the public's belief in our future growth potential at both the revenue and profit lines. After discussions with our new investment banker, we agreed the sale of 20 percent of

CES stock could bring in as much as $5 million. About $3 million of the proceeds would be available for direct investment in CES. The remaining $2 million would be shared among investors and management. If our IPO was successful, CES would be valued in the aggregate at $25 million on the day of its IPO. More importantly, CES would have gained a financial war chest and a publicly traded stock, with which we could begin acquiring distribution forces. Many of us, myself included, relished the idea of going public because we were facing the heavy-expenditure years of college tuitions. The proceeds we would receive from our IPO would certainly help our pocketbooks and put our children through the years of higher education that we had envisioned almost 15 years before when we left the comfort zone of NASA to begin our entrepreneurial journey.

Timing, once again, was crucial. The timing of our offering was significant in that we had negotiated several financially very rewarding customer contracts, which stretched out over the next several years. By late 1980, after a tremendous effort on everyone's part, CES was ready for its public debut. On April 16, 1981, CES became a publicly traded company through a comanaged underwriting conducted by Hambrecht & Quist of California and Baker Watts of Baltimore, Maryland. Both were preeminent investment banking firms at that time.

Chapter Twelve:

Corporate Renewal: Luxury or Necessity?

The mark of a successful man is one who has spent an entire day on the bank of a river without feeling guilty about it.

When CES's sales and profits were exploding, I first became concerned that the corporate performance that we had enjoyed for more than ten years was lessening. Our financial performance was outstanding, but I felt that was largely due to the momentum we had established five years earlier when we initially achieved profitability. Something in my subconscious told me that we were now in the process of losing our momentum. This bothered me because we were still nowhere near the corporate objectives that we had described in our initial business plan, upon which we had raised our initial round of venture capital financing. To meet our objectives in the highly competitive market that we had chosen, my associates and I were going to have to perform well above our peers. Still, there was no concrete proof that we had a problem. It was just a feeling that I had.

I decided to join a corporate networking group for CEOs. I began talking with my peers about my concerns. I found that corporate inertia or lack thereof was something that others had felt, too. It was a classic problem in the business world. It most often occurs when the company's mission becomes diluted because the associates' authority and responsibility, which were initially clear and compelling, is spread across too many people. When that happens, associates no longer feel a strong personal commitment to get the job done. Because CES was so growth determined, we were already experiencing this slack in associates' commitment. As we continued to grow and take on new associates, it would only get worse unless we took some positive action to correct it. But I didn't have any answers. My peers didn't seem to have the answers either.

It was around this time I traveled to England to introduce CES's OCR systems there. We thought the country presented a significant sales opportunity for our products. As I browsed a newsstand before boarding my plane, I bought a recently published book entitled *Top Management Strategy*, by Benjamin Tregoe and John Zimmerman. It was one of the best decisions I have ever made. I devoured the book on my flight. It had a great effect on me then, and it has inspired me tremendously over the years, particularly from a strategic viewpoint. I have used this book as the basis of a long quest to develop a simple, well-defined, easily implemented corporate renewal process. I used the process periodically to reinvigorate CES. I later realized I could use the same process to give other corporations a much-needed boost. The process is described as follows:

A company's strategic statement is the single most important description of an organization, and it should be very carefully crafted. According to Tregoe and Zimmerman, the strategic statement is the "framework that guides the decisions that determine the nature and direction of an organization." [5]It tells what your company is going to do, not how you intend to accomplish it.

Therefore, the first order of business is to determine what the new or freshened corporate strategy should be. This should be decided in the light of the current market as well as operational and financial conditions within the company. Development of the company's strategic statement is difficult, but it's critically important. If you can get this statement right, everything else will begin to fall into place. Armed with your strategic statement, your company will be reinvigorated … at least for another couple years. When you are again hit with a lull in corporate inertia, just start the process all over again.

Where do you go to map out the company's strategic statement? It's best to plan a corporate retreat. Over the years, I have developed a systematic program for corporate retreats. I use it in my current consulting company to great success, and I offer this description to readers as my contribution to your company's success, as I promised in the preface:

Select a retreat location that is off-site, away from all interruptions. But, keep it within a one- to two-hour driving distance. A degree of grandeur helps, too. I have used several hotels on Chesapeake Bay with the meeting room chosen specifically to overlook this beautiful body of water.

If possible, a round conference table is more effective than a rectangular one. Simply, it adds to the equality of the meeting. As the retreat's leader, the CEO uses a protocol called "constructive dissension," described in an Appendix to this book that encourages proactive participation from each attendee by describing specifically why the particular associate has been asked to the retreat. Then that person is challenged to offer his or her opinions. Not surprisingly, the quietest person in the room often makes the most profound contributions. For this reason, I work very hard to get maximum participation. But active participation is often easier to acquire if the attendees have first read *Top Management Strategy*. The leader can suggest this reading beforehand.

A quiet, private dining area should be used to convene the group for dinner on the evening before the retreat actually begins. (Ideally, this same area should be used for the rest of the retreat.) I engage the participants in discussions about themselves, for example, their personal and professional objectives for the next five to ten years. I encourage everyone in the room to speak. This conversation breaks the ice, setting the stage for contributory conversation and indirectly setting the scene for the next day's discussion of the company's future goals.

On the first full day of the retreat, everyone gathers for a round-table discussion on the strengths and weaknesses of all aspects of the company. However, to avoid negativity, participants must name a strength for each weakness. The meeting usually progresses quite well. Constructive dissension becomes an integral part of this session as well as future sessions. The objective of the third session is to reach a unanimous decision among attendees on the choice of a single driving force for the company. This exercise is a great way to understand each other's attitudes and aspirations. It usually pays a high dividend in the company's subsequent operational performance because everyone understands each other a bit or sometimes a whole lot more because of this debate.

In the evening of the first full day of the retreat, while the attendees are relaxing, the CEO usually drafts the initial version of the company's new strategic statement, using the notes that he or she has taken during earlier sessions. The draft strategic statement should be as specific as possible.

The first session of the second day is devoted to the CEO's presentation of the newly crafted strategic statement, posting it on an overhead projector. The CEO then encourages attendees to vigorously dissent, even going as far as the punctuation of the statement as he slowly reads the text, word by word. After about three hours of vigorous debate, attendees will arrive at a mutually acceptable strategic statement for the company … at least until the market or some other force dictates that a change is necessary.

Initially, when we held two-day retreats, I developed a critical agenda during the afternoon of the second day. The critical agenda is a list of the required tasks to fulfill the new strategy. It details who is going to be responsible for each task, the timing of the tasks, and the budget for each item on the list. It also sets up appropriate times to perform interim checks on the progress of each individual task. After holding several retreats, I found that the critical agenda session was just too much to cover without a break of one or two days. The attendees would become so intellectually fatigued by the time that the strategic statement was accepted by all that it was far better to let everyone go home for a long weekend or encourage them to relax in another way, such as playing a round of golf. We'd then reconvene on the following Monday morning at the company to develop the critical agenda.

Over the years, I have modified and added to the retreat process. My recommendation is now that during the week following senior management retreat the critical agenda is firmed up. Everyone then takes a little downtime to recover from the intellectually draining experience of the retreat.

On the second Monday following the retreat, the CEO presents the new or revised strategic statement to the entire company. Over the remainder of that week, all associates meet with their immediate supervisors on an individual or group basis so they can become involved in the company's strategy through in-depth give-and-take discussions of the new strategic statement. By the end of that second week, everyone in the company has become personally involved in the company's new strategic statement. Most importantly, each associate will have had an opportunity to voice his or her views on the new strategy, which encourages everyone to more actively participate in the success of the company. That is critical to your success. Beyond simply drawing a paycheck, every one of the company's associates should have a vested interest in the company's success.

For CES, this meant the granting of five-year, IRS incentive-qualified stock options (ISOs) as well as profit sharing.

The ISOs gave me the opportunity to stand in front my associates and proclaim, "We all own a bit of this rock, and it's up to all of us to turn the bit we own into a little bit of gold!"

CES also enjoyed great success by instituting with board approval profit sharing, that is, 25 percent of corporate profits were set aside to be distributed in proportion to an associate's portion of the company's aggregate annual payroll. I believe this incentive will most probably work at your company, too, regardless of the percentage that is offered. Profit sharing gives your associates a sense of ownership and pride in the company, and that makes them feel good.

The final step in the process is the follow-through, and this step usually gets the least attention. We held a meeting at least quarterly to make sure the critical agenda developed in the renewal process was being fulfilled. This meeting included a progress report that was distributed to all of the associates so everyone would be on the same page.

From today's vantage point, I can see that CES grew so successfully to 1,000 associates, $75 million in revenues, sixteen years of consecutive profitability, five acquisitions, and an increase in the shareholder's original investment of thirty times because we engaged in continuous corporate renewal. In my mind, regular corporate renewal is a necessity for peak performance.

Chapter Thirteen:

Becoming and Running a Public Company

Every problem should be viewed as an opportunity.

After twelve years, we took CES public in 1981. To prepare, several members of our management team and I attended seminars on taking this step. CES consultants and friends with experience had warned us that running a public company was much more difficult than running the same company privately. In retrospect, I must have had cement in my ears because I really never did comprehend the impact of "going public" until we got there.

I like the analogy and believe it to be true that going public is like executing a contract with a New York City department store to decorate their display windows for the Christmas season. After reading the fine print, you find out that you have also committed to decorate the window while stark naked in front of hundreds of gawking spectators.

Going public with our company was uncomfortable. However, for the offering to succeed, CES had to maintain its financial and operational performance while remaining in the corporate limelight. We had to perform despite feeling overwhelmed and very vulnerable. The degree of disclosure that a company is required to make under SEC regulations gives a feeling of intense scrutiny. For me, the process was very intimidating. When our customers saw how much profit CES had accumulated over the past three years as a private company, they would likely be jealous or maybe even angry because they had not enjoyed nearly as much profit as a percentage of sales as CES had reaped over the past several years. This type of complete disclosure, which the SEC required, presented us with the risk that our customer base might disappear before CES had the opportunity to establish itself in its new retail environment.

We took our company public because we believed our new end user sales strategy would support our desired growth in revenue and earnings going forward. We also knew that we were going to compete with several of the same customers who had provided CES with its growth opportunities over the past ten years. If our customers abandoned us before we were ready, sales and profits could suffer severely. The public offering might even fail.

A public company is judged by its shareholders and the general public by what is known to the company's management as the "tyranny of quarter-to-quarter earnings performance." That is, if you miss your projected quarterly earnings number by a penny or two, your stock can plummet precipitously, driving the value of the company down by millions of dollars in a single trading session. This isn't a good way to retain the confidence of your board, stockholders, management, or associates, who control the company's and management's future. During the process of going public, everything the company and you ever did is fair game for due diligence and full disclosure. Attorneys and accountants investigate, check, and recheck everything related to the company. No one, particularly your investment banker who is managing the underwriting, can afford to be embarrassed by something that wasn't fully disclosed in the prospectus.

A highlight of most well-run public offerings is the road show, a multi-city trip that is generally conducted several weeks prior to the scheduled offering date. During the road show week, final presentations are given by management to supporting underwriters, allowing them a chance to personally assess the company so as to encourage them to sell their clients on the idea of investing in the company's IPO.

CES's job was to give these brokers a firsthand opportunity to get comfortable with the company's management. We kept up the road show for a week, one of the most physically and emotionally exhausting weeks of my working life. We traveled to Baltimore, Chicago, San Francisco, Los Angeles, Boston, and New York in just five days. But it also was very exciting because I was able to promote CES, a company I had been leading and building for twelve years. I was very proud of what we had accomplished.

One stop on our road show was of particular note. Our opening presentation in Baltimore had gone very well. The audience saw us as local boys making good. Our plant was only forty miles from the Baltimore Club, where we began our trip. By noon, we were at Faneuil Hall in Boston with one hundred fifty hungry brokers joining us for lunch. Our investment bankers had told us that these brokers would give us no more than forty-five minutes of their time. While they ate, we presented. I felt confident as I began my presentation, but I had no sooner spoken my first sentence when I heard a loud clap of thunder. Faneuil Hall was plunged into darkness, and the microphone went dead. The power was out. I stopped my presentation. The audience could not see or hear me. By the time the power came back on about thirty minutes later, only four brokers were still present. And one was asleep. Fortunately, Boston was our worst experience. From then on, things went well. When we arrived home late on Friday afternoon, we felt we had sold the CES offering. More importantly, our veteran investment bankers felt the same way.

This was a major step for the company, and it was fraught with risk. But even after twelve years in business, eight of them consistently and increasingly profitable, we had to make this major make-or-break decision to fulfill the original corporate and personal objectives that we had set for ourselves.

Please recall that one of the potential problems for CES's public offering was the relationship strain that it might cause with our existing customer base. Because our customer base was limited, each of them absorbed a significant portion of our production. When our prospectus became public, it included every detail of our production allocations, manufacturing costs, general and administrative expenses, compensation of officers and directors, and much more. We had to disclose that we were planning to use our liquid stock and the $3 million raised from the public to acquire

distribution forces that would compete with some of these same customers. Everyone knew that, if we were able to make the leap and take CES
public, we would be free to enter new markets and compete with them.
Not unexpectedly, all hell did break loose. One of our customers even
attempted to disrupt our public offering by spreading negative rumors
relating to our inability to hold our unique competitive position.

Nonetheless, on April 15, 1981, thanks to the persistence of CES management, our investment bankers, lawyers, and accountants, CES became
a publicly traded company, raising $3 million for the company and allow-
ing management to sell another $2 million worth of its shares. The offer-
ing was sold out. Becoming a millionaire, at least on paper, was the
fulfillment of my American Dream. Lynda and I had reached our original
goal that we had set twenty years earlier by acquiring the resources needed
to send our children to college.

I had come a long way in forty-one years. I realized that I didn't reach
this point on my own. Family, teachers, co-workers, friends, and even
competition contributed significantly to my success. Although I've often
used "I" as I have described the birth and growth of CES, a team always
worked with me and backed my every move. Teamwork made CES successful. Every cog in the wheel was important to our success.

Chapter Fourteen:

I Wasn't Careful Enough!

The rate at which a person can mature is directly proportional to the embarrassment he can tolerate.

—Douglas Engelbart

In my other corporate role as the chief salesman for CES, I was constantly looking for potential sales opportunities to increase our manufacturing volume, which would then reduce our manufacturing costs and increase profits.

One day, I heard about an interesting opportunity taking place in Italy that involved the capturing of preprinted bank check information and then transmitting clearing information from remote branches to central clearing banks throughout the country via telephone lines. When I first heard about it, the number of systems was in the thousands. A quick check with the Italian Embassy's Bureau of Internal Economic Affairs in Washington verified there was a mandate to speed the clearing of checks throughout Italy. I further verified that the number of bank branches was in the thousands. A small, moderately fast, exceptionally high-quality OCR reader/transport could provide the answer to Italy's countrywide application. This was a perfect opportunity for CES's OCR reader/transport! But we immediately recognized the reality of a product support problems for systems located in a country that was more than three thousand miles away. Because we didn't even have a sales office or the hundreds of field technicians required to keep our products operating, we needed help to even begin to compete for this potentially lucrative business. CES needed a reputable partner who already had sales and service offices established in Italy. That partner could then purchase the equipment from us at a substantial discount from the retail price. Then they could install and service the equipment over the next five to ten years while we both enjoyed profiting from the relationship.

Only one such independent OCR company quickly came to mind, Recognition Equipment Incorporated (REI). Headquartered in Dallas, REI was then the largest and most respected independent supplier of high-speed OCR reader/transports in the world. REI had offices in all major cities throughout the world, including several in Italy. If we could negotiate a mutually attractive contract with REI, we had a good chance of building and shipping thousands of CES reader/transports. If all came to pass as it might, it would be the largest order ever placed for this type of equipment at that time.

I quickly called REI. After a couple false starts, I located the person in charge of the division responsible for sales in Italy, a man I will call Mr. E. Because of what we believed to be a huge sales opportunity for CES readers in Italy, I quickly arranged to meet Mr. E in Dallas the next week. My first impressions of Mr. E were that he was handsome, intelligent, smooth, experienced, and an ideal person to be in a senior marketing/sales role in the world's leading independent OCR company.

I became even more impressed with Mr. E as we worked together to develop a multifaceted plan to bring our two companies together in what appeared to be an attractive and mutually profitable way to capture a large part of the Italian remote check-processing opportunity. This was a wonderful opportunity!

Over the next several months, Mr. E and I got together numerous times. Mr. E met CES's senior management. Everyone, Lynda included, was impressed with the dynamic, experienced, smooth, and sophisticated presence of this tall Texan. We also were fond of his wife. In fact, Mr. E's family and mine became so close that, when he and his wife would visit Maryland, they would be guests in our home.

As our business and personal relationship developed, I decided that Mr. E might make a nice catch for CES in our quest to expand into different markets and geographic regions. In addition, Mr. E's industry background, business relationships, and résumé would dress up our public offering prospectus by demonstrating that we could attract and recruit the best of the best from companies that were far larger than CES. It would add a lot to our credibility, especially on the eve of our public offering.

One Saturday evening, when Mr. E and his wife were in town, we invited them, along with CES's senior management and their wives, to our house for dinner. I wanted everyone to get to know each other socially, as well as at work. At the end of the evening, I quietly asked my associates for their views on Mr. E. Each gave me a hearty thumbs-up signal on Mr. E's joining us as the senior vice president of marketing at CES. Later that night, Mr. E and I discussed salary, stock options, and general responsibilities. We shook hands on the deal as Mr. E gave his verbal assent.

The next day, along with our wives, Mr. E and I began looking for a house for Mr. and Mrs. E in our rural community. We found one that same day. Mr. E submitted an offer and a deposit. I was sure I had found my backup, just in case I could not run a publicly traded company.

The next day, I went to work exhilarated. I could not wait to tell CES board members, our underwriting investment bankers, and my associates at CES about our weekend's recruiting success. The first order of business, however, was to call the printers, who were setting type to produce thousands of copies of our final public offering prospectus. Mr. E's acceptance of the role of vice president of marketing in CES was a material fact that, under SEC rules, required immediate disclosure. Needless to say, I was delighted to make this disclosure. Copies of our prospectus were expected to be shipped later that same day to waiting brokers across the country. After completing the draft of my description of Mr. E's illustrious background, I sent the announcement of this great hire via fax to our board and to the media as I believed that it could only benefit CES if this information was widely broadcasted. Then I prepared and sent an employment contract to Mr. E codifying the employment terms we had agreed upon with a handshake forty-eight hours earlier. As the morning progressed, I began receiving jubilant responses to my earlier faxes. Everyone was excited and complimented us on attracting and capturing such an outstanding addition to our team.

I then packed and left for a previously scheduled sales trip. I also planned to stop in Dallas on the return leg of my trip to pick up the executed employment agreement from Mr. E as we attempted to move the REI negotiations for the Italian order closer to conclusion.

While on my trip to northern California, I received a phone call at seven o'clock in the morning from a senior vice president of REI.

"Brian," he said excitedly, "I have some very disheartening news for both of us. I have your prospectus in front of me. I see that Mr. E has decided to join you as your senior vice president of marketing."

"Ouch!" I thought. "This guy is going to give me hell for stealing his favorite, fair-haired boy."

"Brian," he continued, "I only learned yesterday that Mr. E has been triple dipping. He's been drawing a salary here at REI. He's working for a start-up computer company here in Dallas, as its president, at night and on weekends. Now I see that he's accepted a third position with you at CES."

I thought, "I can't believe what I am hearing!"

The vice president said, "Here's the name and telephone number for the chairman of the computer company. You and I have trouble, my friend."

REI's vice president and I were both caught off guard. We each had felt that we had Mr. E's total commitment. Not only was that wrong, but Mr. E also had a third company to which he was committed. And I had just announced in our prospectus and through the media Mr. E's new position at CES. This was much worse than dropping a $1.7 million check in the toilet!

I was in such shock that I could only thank the vice president for calling and hung up.

I thought, "How could this have happened?"

I decided I needed to take a run to try to clear my head. By the time I returned, I had only slightly collected myself, but it was enough to know that my first duty was to verify the information that REI's vice president had given me. I felt my best source was the chairman of the third company. Once I identified myself, my counterpart erupted in rage against Mr. E, saying he had betrayed all of us. The president was most empathetic to my problem at CES. We commiserated for a few moments, and it was very clear; I had my verification.

I immediately called Bob McLaughlin, my old friend and corporate attorney.

He only said, "Jeepers, (a term that I knew Bob reserved for use only for his most serious concerns) we have real problems."

He then suggested that we needed to get the bad news out early. We would prepare a five- to fifteen-line description of the event that contradicted statements made in the original prospectus, produced and distributed only a day before. We would then distribute this correction immediately. CES was about to look quite foolish. I felt terrible about our blunder. Company management's credibility is always a major factor in presenting oneself to the public in an IPO. For CES, this had to be one of the all-time goofs. It required retraction of significant material facts within forty-eight hours of publication.

I then placed a personal phone call to Mr. E. Weeping, he tried to describe the tangled web of deceit he had created and in which he finally had been caught. But I didn't want to hear his excuses for his unethical behavior. I was really calling just to be certain the facts were correct. And they were. He had deceived three different companies by promising to be completely committed to each one. With that, our relationship was over. I haven't spoken to or heard from Mr. E in the twenty-six years since that phone call.

I cut my sales trip short. I flew home that morning to face embarrassment, accusations of naïveté, failure, and customer ridicule. I wasn't sure what I'd have to endure. But the long flight home gave me a chance to gain a degree of perspective. I decided to employ a formula that had worked for me in Boston fifteen years earlier. I'd get the bad news out, apologize, and work to put things right.

I spent the next days on the phone, calling everyone to whom I owed an explanation. I told them that I had been duped. Amazingly, maybe because the situation was so bad on so many fronts, I received an outpouring of unexpected sympathy. In fact, a sufficient number of understanding financial analysts, brokers, and purchasing shareholders forgave CES so we were able to continue the process of our public offering.

Incidentally, although the Italian application was a very good one, bureaucracy and politics precluded success in that arena. We only sold fifty units before the whole idea went bust.

Chapter Fifteen:

Growth through Mergers

The stock market is obsessed with growth; ignore this fact at your peril.

A saying goes, "When in Rome, do as the Romans do." In CES's newly positioned status as a public company, we knew the stock market was obsessed with growth, including growth in sales, profits, earnings/share in market share, and just about anything that can be legitimately construed to imply a pattern of growth. Investors pay a handsome price in terms of price/earnings multiples for companies that have clearly demonstrated their understanding of growth. All public companies and even conservative private enterprises commonly state to protect themselves from stockholder suits that *"past performance should not be an indication of investors" future expectations."* However, in the real world of corporate competition, one of the major indicators that investors use to measure a company's ability to grow is its past performance. If you ignore this fact, your stock will likely suffer. If you pay attention to growth and make long-term growth decisions, you can enjoy a strong financial ride. CES had experienced tremendous growth success over the previous five years at the revenue line and even more so at the profit line, which was the reason why we were able to achieve our successful IPO.

Two types of growth most often apply to corporate organizations: organic and inorganic.

- **Organic growth** is demonstrated when a company is built one step at a time. Growth is achieved through internal development that is, spending precious R&D dollars in a very controlled and effective manner. In football terms, organic growth means marching down the field three or four yards at a time, grinding out a touchdown. It's a safer and surer way to go. CES had succeeded with organic growth.

- **Inorganic growth**, or acquisition growth, may be likened to a Hail Mary pass in football. The ball is thrown down the field so the team can score quickly and decisively. In the corporate world, inorganic growth can be very exciting, but it's usually quite risky because it involves the integration of two different cultures and that can be quite difficult.

CES had been developing and effectively selling unique technology during the previous decade of spectacular growth through the creation of unique, cost-effective, highly specialized products for the RP market. Within this product market, CES had also created a specialized printing device called an MICR printer that is used for generalized check and RP applications. For example, it's recognizable by those funny-looking little symbols found at the bottom of all corporate and personal checks. Through these markings, high-speed machines read and sort checks. Thanks to our public offering, CES now had the financial resources to pursue additional new products much more aggressively. In a stock market that was relatively well-disposed to high-tech stocks, CES was positioned to attract the interest of corporations who possessed what we needed, that is, retail sales and service forces with excellent existing customer relationships. Given our technology and the relative disarray of the RP market, CES management decided the company should bear the greater risk of pursuing growth through acquisitions, that is, inorganic growth, while it continued its traditional organic growth. This would enable us to take full and immediate advantage of the state of our technology and at the same time gain important customer relationships.

We used previously developed contacts at specific companies to ascertain the attitude of each company's senior management toward a possible merger with CES. In general we would propose that CES purchase the distribution and field/service force from the target company in exchange for stock in CES. Thus, sellers would acquire publicly traded stock, which they could either cash in or hold for longer-term appreciation. Thus, we went down both roads believing that the combination of our superior products, distribution, and service meant that CES's profits would grow substantively. As such, our stock would appreciate, benefiting CES's and the target companies' shareholders through perceived and actual growth.

Over the next decade, CES acquired five companies and produced a 25 percent compound rate of annualized growth in revenue while continuing to produce above-average profits. CES prospered under its "growth by acquisition" strategy, even as it continued its treasured organic R&D growth.

The work involved with mergers and acquisitions is very complex and time-consuming. There is abundant opportunity to make mistakes. We developed the following guidelines for CES's approach to growth through mergers, recognizing that each merger is unique and must be treated as such.

Primary Thoughts

Our experience taught us that the single most important aspect of any merger is the creation of a detailed post-merger operational plan (PMOP) for the merged companies. After our first nearly disastrous acquisition experience at CES, we decided that both sides of the potential merger partners needed to develop a detailed five-year business plan before closing the transaction. We insisted that the plan detail the responsibilities, authority, and projected expectations of every individual who was to remain with the newly formed and combined organizations. Representatives from both CES and the company under consideration had to learn to plan together to improve the merger's chances of success before the closing occurred. We came to believe that the PMOP is the key operational tool if the success ratios for mergers and acquisition statistics are to improve.

Further Thoughts and Ideas on Mergers

There is a difference between acquisitions and mergers. From the beginning of discussions with a potential merger candidate, ensure the candidate knows what you know about what the candidate is bringing to the table and its value. Don't make the company you are trying to merge with feel like an abandoned dog that you are generously picking up from the animal shelter. To proactively establish the fact that you recognize the synergistic potential of the companies, call the transaction a "merger" rather than an acquisition. This lends dignity to the candidate company. You only need to be slightly better than the competition and have a good relationship-based sales force that can convey this superiority and thus win the lion's share of the business. Success depends on the mental attitude of the entire workforce—old and new. It needs to start with the title, that is, a "merger," that you give to the transaction.

A merger is like an iceberg. Only one-third of what needs to be done to make the transaction a success is initially apparent. This is why the planning step described previously is so important. A merger begins with relentless pressure from all sides to get the deal done. It involves the necessary presence of lawyers, accountants, and bankers who also want to complete the transaction. Management must be keenly sensitive to the fact that, beyond the high level of intense activity, there remains at least two-thirds more operational work that will have to done if the merger is to meet expectations.

Mergers ultimately succeed because of the people involved. Make every effort to ensure that management and the associates of the company being merged with feel positive and involved in the transaction. Use multiple goal-setting meetings, profit sharing and stock option awards, and continued contact among the associates of both companies to reduce negative feelings, improve attitudes, and create an atmosphere of trust and cooperation.

Mergers are an opportunity to reinvigorate both old and new associates with the company's mission. To accomplish this objective, two features are key to its success: ownership and management participation in the newly combined company. Ownership can be effected through a stock option plan that allows associates to earn a certain number of options each year, usually over a period of five years. Participation is accomplished by frequent communication meetings. At each such meeting, senior management solicits answers to two fundamental questions. How can we improve our products and services for our customers? And how can we make this company a more efficient and desirable place to work?

Many of the answers to these questions can come from those who labor in the company for years but rarely get an opportunity to voice their opinions. Pose these questions at quarterly meetings. Then make yourself available to your associates by walking around the company to listen to those who were not comfortable speaking in front of others at the meeting. After building the necessary trust relationship with all of your associates, the answers to these two questions can work wonders for your company, as they did for CES.

In my experience, it's important to meet often with my associates and increase the frequency of the meetings when conditions at the company are uncertain. I recommend meeting with your associates at least quarterly. Tell it like it is. Always leave them with an honest assessment of the future of the company. Preparing for such meetings will also help you measure how well your company is doing. You can't do this enough. Providing legitimate hope for the future should be one of management's highest priorities. Hope can help to dispel fear and increase productivity.

By their very nature, mergers are disruptive to all company workers but especially concerned are those company customers who have chosen a supplier who has now been merged into another company. Within this real concern is a tremendous opportunity for the merged company. The CEO, the senior salesperson assigned to the account, and the head of customer support should meet with customers to reassure them that the merged company will meet their needs in the future. Do not miss this crucial window of opportunity to keep all the customers available to the merged company. Otherwise, their anxiety may take them elsewhere.

For CES, the period from 1981 to 1989 was one of continuously searching for new merger candidates, negotiating transactions, and integrating the new partner company or division into CES's successful business.

Chapter Sixteen:

The Sale of CES

It's important to know your own and your company's limits.

With extraordinary long-term support from the CES board of directors, associates, investors, and bankers, we had raised CES from a newborn to adolescence and to a state of early maturity. We were approaching $100 million in revenue. We had a thousand associates, and we had been quite profitable for more than sixteen years. On multiple occasions during this period of success, my partners and I had been asked if we were interested in selling the company. My obligation to our investors and associates, as well as to my own desires, required me to give every such question serious consideration. I asked potential buyers to put the offer in writing. Essentially, I said, "Make us an offer we can't refuse." And I'd take it to the board. The potential buyer usually wanted an estimate of our price, so I'd ask him or her to execute a Nondisclosure/Confidentiality Agreement (NDA) and once they did I would share our five-year business plan, which projected our growth expectations in revenue and profits as well as internal development plans. I also shared our estimates of what the going price was for companies in our field with similar performance and expectation levels. In most cases, this approach positioned CES comfortably for negotiations on a rational basis, and we didn't need to say yes or no to provide an on-the-spot yes or no answer to the inquirer.

Because our growth had been so spectacular with revenue up at a 25 percent compound rate of growth, it was reasonable for us to use a high multiple of future sales and profits to justify the selling price for the company. The high price we were asking assumed we could maintain the momentum we had demonstrated in preceding years. Most times, however, the price was higher than the prospective buyer was able or wanted to pay.

One of the companies that continuously inquired about CES was Texas-based BancTec. For fifteen years, CES had been a critical product supplier to them. BancTec had gone public a few years before CES, and it had maintained a continuing interest in effecting a merger. Both companies believed a merger might be possible because BancTec needed CES's patented MICR encoder. Additionally, BancTec still had a large share of the cash proceeds from its own public offering available for acquisition purposes. No one else, including IBM, NCR, and Burroughs, had been able to master the MICR printing technology at CES's price/performance ratio for the particular application that BancTec had used to build its own successful business. Credit for this MICR product goes, once again, to CES's superb engineering team led by John Guthrie.

We asked ourselves, "Where do we go from here?"

We had speculated that capturing more of the RPS market would become increasingly difficult because competitors who wished to remain in the field would desperately try to avoid losing more market share to CES. Our competitors would cut prices and offer special deals to secure an order, which made it very difficult for CES to hold the cherished margins that produced the earnings required to stimulate interest in our stock. To continue our growth momentum, CES would have to find new markets. Because we believed that we should plan our future in orders of magnitude, we foresaw that getting to a $1 billion in revenue, which was about ten times where we were at that time, would require a substantial change in the human resources at CES, as well as the product composition that CES produced.

Despite CES restructuring sections of the company multiple times over the years, I didn't think we were up to making the substantial changes required to take the company to this particular revenue mark. I was also not willing to take the risk of turning the company over to someone else.

We looked at a number of opportunities and measured the risk/reward potential for each. We gradually concluded that this might be a good time to encourage those who had shown previous interest in acquiring CES to come forward with offers.

When evaluating the complexities of whether or not to sell, at least three main groups must be considered: the shareholders, the company's associates, and management's desires. The question to be answered is simple. How much is enough for each of these entities? CES shareholders, particularly the early investors, had done very well. Original investors were positioned to receive a return that was thirty-four times their investment. Many of our associates held stock options that would reward them in the 5 to 10X range for their hard work, if a sale occurred.

On the personal side, Lynda and I wrestled with the question for several months before we decided that the answer remained with our lifestyle objectives for our senior years. By 1989, only one of our children remained in college. We were living comfortably on our fifteen-acre minifarm, where we raised livestock. We had achieved our original educational goals for our children, and we had a lifestyle that was beyond our dreams. We were both quite happy, and we had lived an exciting life during CES's years of trial and success. We needed to answer one other question. How much money do we need for the future? The answer that we came up with was: we needed enough money to maintain our lifestyle as it was until our Maker decided to call us home. I never contemplated stopping work. I just wanted to remove some of the relentless pressure that I had experienced for more than twenty years. I wanted to slow down a bit. If we could get a price for CES that was close to what I thought the company should sell for, everyone who mattered would come out just fine.

So, as we approached the end of our twentieth year in business, we reviewed where CES had been, where we were, and where we wanted to go. We had many reasons to be proud of CES, including the quality of our products, the innovative solutions we had devised for our customers, and most of all, the real value we brought to our customers by reducing their costs for labor, improving their transaction accuracy, and expediting the flow of collected cash into their depository accounts. CES was a financial success. We dominated our niche market by selling more than half of the RP units sold to the market in 1988. In fact, since 1985, no knowledgeable person in the industry would seriously consider buying RP equipment without at least considering a bid from CES. Both the organic and inorganic growth strategies had worked for CES, and we were at the top of our game. During the first twelve years of CES's life, we created $25 million in corporate value, as evidenced by the price that investors paid for our stock on the day we took the company public. This translates to the creation of an average of $2.1 million per year for the first twelve years of our life. During the last eight years, as a public company, we added another $19 million to our value for an average of $2.4 million per year, evidenced by finally selling CES for $44 million in 1989. On the other hand, CES's inorganic growth was a lot more exciting and challenging for many of us.

In any case, and with some mixed emotion, we decided to take the idea of selling CES to our board. After much discussion, they unanimously supported putting the company up for sale. We hired a Wall Street mergers and acquisitions firm to help us locate potential buyers. After several meetings with potential buyers, the most interested and aggressive suitor was BancTec. Negotiations with BancTec took four months, but we finally closed the deal.

Quantitatively, a post-sale analysis showed that, in twenty years, the CES team had turned Jim Melcher's 1968 initial investment of $300,000 into an aggregate company value of $44 million of which Jim had been able to preserve 25 percent ownership for FVF or $10.5 million for a gain of more than 30X his fund's original investment!

Put another way, if you had invested in CES on the day we started at Jim Melcher's price and had stayed for the duration, you would have doubled your money every two and half years. Our last major investors were the public, those who came in eight years before the sale to BancTec. In those eight years, CES's value grew from $25 million to $44 million. CES's growth strategies had worked to everyone's benefit.

Qualitative successes of the company are more difficult to measure. The incredible teamwork based on trust and cooperation made CES a place where people wanted to work because they enjoyed working there.

Management worked hard to ensure that everyone participated in the day-to-day management of the company. Additionally, management further enhanced returns to associates by offering stock options to as many associates as we were allowed under ever-changing and SEC regulations.

When I was in my late teens and early twenties, I served in the United States Navy aboard a submarine. Comradeship and responsibility were a way of life as well as an essential ingredient for survival. I'm proud to say that we were able to create a similar environment at CES. I owe that success to each and every person who was a part of our twenty-year journey. It was, for all of us, a tremendous experience as we were able to live out our version of the American Dream.

Chapter Seventeen:

Ideal Characteristics of the Entrepreneurial Leader

A real entrepreneur is someone who has no safety net underneath him.

—Henry Kravis

Several of Never Give Up!'s early reviewers suggested that I provide a list of what I considered to be the most important characteristics of a winning entrepreneur's personality. My first reaction was that there are already at least one hundred such pretty good lists readily available, so how can I make a difference?

I begin with a factual account of my 1967 attempt to come to grips with what such a list might look like. I vividly remember waking in a cold sweat one night, while on a family vacation in Madison, Connecticut. That was the same summer that I had accepted the position of CEO for what was to become CES, and I needed to figure out a job description for myself. The facts were that I was quite intimidated by my new job even though I didn't even know what it entailed! And well I should have been! In looking over the list below, I had less than one-third of the characteristics that I am describing as important, and I certainly didn't know how to develop myself to become proficient at the remaining two-thirds of the list. So what follows is not just a list but the methods I evolved over the years to overcome my shortcomings, which I hope will show readers a path which will ease the pain that I went through in developing the solution over twenty-five years.

Also, this list is no particular order with the exception of the first characteristic, Unconditional Honesty, which must be pursued relentlessly because it's the one characteristic where forgiveness is not usually forthcoming. The remaining fourteen characteristics, important as they may seem to be, are dependent upon where you and your company are on your journey. This said, my ideal list follows:

- Unconditional Honesty

- Driven by Legitimate Passion

- Appropriate Educational Background

- Appreciation of Organizational Development

- High Energy Level

- Availability of a Distracting Hobby

- Inordinate Persistence

- Close Spousal or Significant Other Support

- Relevant Experience in a Similar Venture

- Sales Personality

- Diligent in His/her Work Ethic

- Global Visionary

- Compassion

- Reasonably High Risk Tolerance

- Lifelong Learner

The Problems with This List

Rarely are investors or corporate boards presented with the opportunity to select leaders to run their businesses with someone so gifted as to have all of these characteristics fully developed.

As I look at this list, I grant that it's intimidating! If I had been presented with such a list in 1967, I might have never started. The good news is that you don't have to have all of these capabilities to start, but you do have to make a commitment to gradually develop these capabilities over time, prioritizing the schedule so that it best fits your company's needs. The time to begin is now, so let's get started:

Unconditional Honesty

I wasn't born honest. In fact, I distinctly remember the exhilaration and satisfaction that I gleaned as a young boy when I was able to swipe something from our neighborhood candy store. When I was caught, my mother would lecture me and then punish me. In retrospect, those lectures finally took their toll on my wanton habits and set me straight.

Much later, as I entered the business world as a naïve, gullible rookie, I began to realize that to be successful, I could only afford to work with or compete with people who were as honest as I had become. Otherwise, I'd most probably lose.

My mother had told me in one of those many lectures, "Oh, what a tangled web we weave when first we practice to deceive."

As I grew, I decided that Mom was right. If I wanted successful outcomes, I had better act accordingly and carefully watch my ethics as well as those of my co-workers and competitors.

Based on my mother's influence and my early business experience, I adopted a lifelong policy of immediately breaking off a sale, relationship, negotiation, or engagement of any kind if I felt the person with whom I was dealing wasn't unconditionally honest.

I suggest that the best approach is to carefully study the probable long-term outcome of living a life of unconditional honesty versus a course of even partial dishonesty. My life's study clearly shows me that unconditional honesty is always the best policy at work, at home, and at play. In business, constructive dissension is a way to determine unconditional honesty because it's often necessary to research the truth or ethics of a situation to get the clearest picture of how to proceed.

Driven by Legitimate Passion

In the world of business, passion is equivalent to having a twelfth man on a football team. Passion provides that extra competitive advantage that a company needs to develop products and beat its competitors. Proactive development of passion in yourself and your associates is an important part of a CEO's job description. To have a passion for your work, you must have commitment, attitude, planning, and persistence, or CAPP. Each of these elements needs special attention.

Put forth your best effort to develop your own and your corporation's passion by organizing seminars where you, as the leader, can stimulate your associates to find a way to be passionate about their work. Passion should be a part of every associate's job description and a part of every associate's review. At least once a year, associates should work together with their supervisor to develop passion for their work.

Appropriate Educational Background

Education, whether it's achieved through informal or formal means, is a vitally important contributor to an entrepreneur's ultimate success. Most importantly, you should have learned the value of careful study of available alternatives. I didn't start out believing this. In fact, during grade school and high school, I probably averaged a "C"performance, at best. But I did ultimately reach a turning point that helped me to see the value and importance of education.

At my mother's insistence, after high school, I started college on a trial basis. At that time, any resident of my home state who was a graduate of an accredited high school had a right to a trial semester at our state university. I quickly found the "bad" crowd, and I got involved in activities like fraternity beer parties, dating, and sports, giving little attention to what should have been my primary goal: pursuit of academics. Forty-three days after the start of fall semester, I was summoned with my parents to the dean's office to review my performance. The stern-looking dean pulled out a lengthy description of my inattention and mischief and advised my parents that, if they withdrew me from the university that very day, he would tear up the damaging record of my college experience thus far. And if he did this, perhaps someday, when I grew up, I might be admitted to another college.

My mother and father were, of course, embarrassed and angry. As far as they were concerned, another college wasn't an option. They informed me that I'd be joining the Navy and I had no choice in the matter.

A few weeks later I found myself on a train to a Navy boot camp. The primary goal of boot camp is to learn how to respond to orders and more orders. This inevitably wears thin. About halfway through boot camp, I saw an advertisement for the submarine service.

"Volunteer for the submarine service! You'll receive hazardous duty pay, and you'll enjoy the best chow that the armed services can provide!"

I decided to apply. In hindsight, I really didn't know what I was doing, in volunteering for the claustrophobic conditions of living in a small tube with seventy-eight other men. However, in retrospect, the submarine service was easily the smartest thing that I could have done at that time in my life. Upon acceptance of my application, I was put through a series of physical, intellectual, and emotional tests used to determine my suitability for life aboard a submarine. While the tests were somewhat exhausting, the results were positive. Upon graduation from boot camp, I was ordered to go to submarine school in New London, Connecticut.

As soon as I arrived at our submarine base, the testing stated all over again. These tests were intended to weed out those who could not make the grade before the Navy spent a lot of money on training them. When I passed again, I was relieved. Now, as we waited for a full class to accumulate, we spent our time learning how to escape from a downed submarine.

Students were gathered in a classroom and introduced to the escape procedure. First, by splashing around on the surface, we were to familiarize ourselves with the escape tank, a 40 ft diameter X 100 ft high structure full of water. Next, we descended by elevator to the 10-ft, 25-ft, 50-ft and finally the 100-ft depth levels. At each level Navy frog men coached us on how to don our escape gear and ascend to the surface. The instructions seemed simple enough until the instructors pointed out that the pressure at 100 ft was such that the body and lungs could explode unless we correctly learned to unload the excess volume of air as we ascended. On the other hand, if we ascended too quickly, our blood could essentially boil and we would get the bends, which could cause an excruciating death or paralysis. Clearly, paying attention, learning and practicing the correct procedure was critically important to my life's continued well-being. I also began to realize that joking time was over and I had better shape up.

Following a successful graduation from submarine-escape training, we began the actual classroom work for submarine school. Because I had never learned to properly study in grade school and/or high school, I was having a rough time and I quickly fell behind in my class. I was actually in danger of flunking out. I needed to raise my average score, which was computed after every Friday's written exam. I decided that after all I had come through to get to this point in my pursuit of the coveted dolphin insignia worn by qualified submariners, failure in the classroom wasn't an option. I could not and would not fail! For the first time in my life, I felt a real need to step up to the academic plate. I attended after-hours sessions with the instructors, who seemed more than willing to help students who really wanted help. Over the sixteen-week training school period, I grabbed hold of a missing element of my life, that is, pursuit of academic excellence. When I later returned to college after a two-year tour in the Navy, I had finally matured enough to fully appreciate the benefits of education. I made the dean's list for superior academic performance multiple times. I owe this performance to my short but effective Navy career.

Since that time, I have never given up my desire to be a good student. Although I took many classes in college, that prepared me for a physics degree and my technical career at the Naval Ordnance Laboratory and NASA, I wasn't equipped, educationally, for the business world. To successfully compete in the business world, I once again had to return to the classroom to learn. And that's exactly what I did.

Private industry, government, and educational institutions provide multiple opportunities for evening and weekend learning experiences that will equip you with the specific tools necessary to succeed in your career. The American Management Association, Dale Carnegie, Sandler Associates, and many others provide tremendous short-term learning experiences. These resources, coupled with on-the-job training, allowed me to make the transition from physicist to salesman to CEO. You can do the same as long as you never ever give up.

Appreciation of Organizational Development

Once an idea has been hatched and vetted, the most important thing you can do as an entrepreneur is develop a plan by which you can maximize return for both the short- and long-term for yourself and your associates. For example, develop a five-year business plan, including the organization, strategy, mission, operational plans, and financials, that is, income, cash flow, and balance sheet statements. Keep in mind that an organization is only as strong as its weakest link. Above all else, take plenty of time to get the right people in the right slots by carefully studying each of your colleagues. The Myers-Briggs Type Indicator (MBTI) is a good way to evaluate personality type. Be sure the positions they assume play to their strengths and avoid their weaknesses. Also be sure the position fits within their definition of their workplace passion.

When I was CEO of CES, one of the most difficult tasks I faced was requesting resignations from well-intentioned associates who simply could not grow to the higher levels of performance that a successful, growth-determined company required. I was so determined to fix immediate organizational problems with someone who could help at the moment that I failed to look out for the five- and ten-year prognosis on that individual's growth potential. While this isn't an easy thing to assess, I believe I could have done a better job of reviewing potential by asking candidates during the interview process to prepare a job description for both the current position as described to them as well as what that position would look like at ten times its current responsibility level.

As to the company's business plan, it is my contention that this is a three- to six-month effort. It shouldn't be done in a vacuum. Whenever possible, involve the other principles. This means responsibilities are assigned. Thus, it begins the process of building the organization. Your baseline structure will probably last a long time, so take whatever time you need to make it as right as possible. It can be tough to change.

To get in touch with and stay on top of your organization's development, read *The Daily Drucker* by Peter F. Drucker or *Good to Great* by John Collins. These books are full of organizational wisdom.

High Energy Levels

As a child, my parents told me that I was always far too energetic for their tastes. This entrepreneurial characteristic probably came to me from deep within my genes. As I approached my late twenties I came to believe that vigorous exercise begets more energy, and I undertook what has become a lifetime habit of running two to four miles every other day. This regimen has paid high dividends, both in my energy level and ability to relax because of the endorphin effect. When stimulated by vigorous exercise, relaxation hormones are released, which bring about calmness while providing increased amounts of energy.

Your diet will also contribute to your success as an entrepreneur. In my case, I have been lucky enough to have had two very health-conscious and exercise-driven spouses who constantly and benevolently watched over my eating habits. If you don't have such a significant other, make a deal with someone close to you so you will be constantly aware of each other. Meet at least once a month to report your exercise and diet program progress.

Availability of a Distracting Hobby

As an entrepreneur, try and have or develop a hobby that is so enjoyable or distracting that your mind becomes preoccupied, giving you time to relax. Your hobby can be anything that you like. It just needs to fulfill the job of being distracting. It should also be fun, and it should easily fit into your lifestyle.

Inordinate Persistence

By far, persistence is the most important characteristic in an entrepreneur's tool kit. Looking back on my business and personal life, I can recall many situations that looked so hopeless that it would have been easier to just give up. Why did I stay the course? A combination of pride, ego, fear, and belief in what we were doing coalesced in my mind and heart to produce my personal mantra of never ever giving up.

My explanation as to how and why this works is quite simple. Unless one is impaired, we all learn by doing. Each time we do something, we get increasingly better at it. This also validates the maxim, "If you can survive, you will thrive!" In any case, persistence is the one-word formula that has always worked for me!

Close Support

You may have heard, "Behind every good man is a great woman." I believe this is true, but it's also true that a great man is behind every good woman. It takes a team to win. One of your most valuable team members can be the person who is closest to you, that is, your spouse or significant other. This doesn't mean that you will rely on that person's every word, but that you should carefully analyze his or her strengths and weaknesses and listen very carefully, when they are speaking from one of their positions of strength. It's lonely at the top. Having a trusted confidant at home is one of the surest ways to ease the burdens of your leadership responsibilities.

Relevant Experience in a Similar Venture

If you're inexperienced, as I was when I started my entrepreneurial journey, try to locate a veteran entrepreneur, one with whom you feel comfortable. Be sure the person you choose as your mentor actually has the necessary experience. Look for someone who has a baseline of experiences that meet or exceed your projected corporate objectives. Consider getting together regularly with like-minded business executives. Just telling your problems to an experienced ear can help quite a bit.

Sales Personality

I advocate this characteristic because, in my own years as a CEO, I believe I spent 98 percent of my time in selling my ideas to my board, investors, associates, and customers. Learning from Dale Carnegie, Sandler Associates, or any qualified sales training group sure beats learning on the job. Get this training early. It will start paying dividends immediately.

Diligence in Work Ethic

"First to arrive, last to leave" is a good axiom for a CEO to follow. It sets the right tone for associates and lets them know that the CEO really cares about the company where they work.

In addition, frequent formal and informal communications sparks performance. Meet at least quarterly with your associates. Truthfully advise them where you believe the company has been, is now, and hopes to go over the next year. Make yourself available in the week that follows through a process called "management by walking around." Associates need to know that you are approachable. Over time and after gaining a trusting relationship with you, they likely will find ways of conveying messages to you that will spur you on to better manage your own company.

Global Visionary

One of the primary responsibilities of a CEO is to ensure the long-term vision, stability, and growth of the organization. You may find it necessary to allocate specific times away from the office, either at home or some place of grandeur, to lift your thinking beyond the pressures of day-to-day activities. To me, it's important to "set the mood." On the night before my morning away from the office, I'd try to read a chapter or two in books like *Megatrends* by John Naisbitt or something by Peter Drucker. I also frequently questioned myself on the status of the company or asked myself how we could raise our revenue. On a quarterly basis, I'd also compel myself to consider the need for a corporate retreat for senior management in our company. For more information on this activity, see Chapter Twelve.

Another successful tool that I used was to establish a product-planning group, that is, a select group of individuals from within the company who possess special, globally oriented sensitivities to products and services that fit within your corporate mission. This group is charged with the responsibility of providing the concepts and detailed specifications for products that your company will be producing two to five years in the future.

Essentially, visionary planning is one of many jobs for which an entrepreneurial leader is responsible, but it can't be done in a vacuum. You will need to organize this important function by drawing on the best talent available in the organization.

Another major contributor to drawing exceptional talent is a policy of sharing the credits the organization deserves as well as sharing its wealth of ownership through multiyear stock option grants. CES received a big payoff for sharing ownership with its associates.

For information on employee stock ownership plans, visit the National Center for Employee Ownership Web site at www.nceo.org.

Compassion

Compassion means you "show feelings of sympathy for the suffering of others, often with a desire to help." I like this standard definition and the concept of helping others. Eventually, all of us find ourselves in need of some sort of help. In my experience, the higher you go in an organization, the more compassionate the person.

Compassion also presents an opportunity to affirm someone's misfortune, which usually serves to build a deeper, long-term mutual respect. I tried to ensure that CES associates felt comfortable with our company and in their roles within the company. This action served me and CES well over its twenty-year life.

Reasonably High risk Tolerance

You can't get very far in life without taking some degree of risk. The question is: how much risk should I, we take? It's part of the leader's job to constantly engage in the leadership of projects, some of which are, by their very nature, reasonably risky. Ask yourself if the risk is foolhardy and then answer the question by becoming familiar with a process called "Monte Carlo Analysis," which quantifies risk and, even more important, points you in the direction of reducing your risk through specific courses of action on particular elements of the project under consideration.

Lifelong Learner

Accept the fact that life of a leader on an entrepreneurial journey is a relentless pursuit of intellectual activity and is a necessary part of the landscape. Constant reading, attendance at short courses, and promotion of a corporate learning environment can contribute substantively to your peak performance and your company's. It's natural to be happy when you learn something new and empowering. Why shouldn't you proactively pursue learning as one of the differentiating characteristics of your corporation?

Peter Drucker once described the spirit of an organization by noting the inscription on Andrew Carnegie's tombstone, "Here lies a man who knew how to enlist in his service better men than himself."

In a similar vein, Drucker noted a slogan he'd seen, which related to a campaign to find jobs for the physically handicapped: "It's the abilities, not the disabilities that count."[6]

Figure out what each of your associates' strengths are. Help them to develop these strengths so they can perform more effectively. Finally, never ever give up.

Chapter Eighteen:

What Will I Do Now?

Entrepreneurs should be able to recognize when it's time to move on to their next thing!

The day that the acquisition agreement with BancTec was closed was my last day at CES. While I had been prepared to stay on, the new owners felt it best for all concerned that I leave. In retrospect, this was probably good for both parties. I suspect I'd have been in a continuous battle with the new owners over how to run the company.

Immediately after the closing, I decided I needed a total break to regain my equilibrium. Earlier in my life, I had enjoyed the refreshing lift that outdoor activity gave me. I looked at several options and finally settled on two possibilities: the Outward Bound program and the National Outdoor Leadership School (NOLS). Either would bring a fresh and invigorating perspective for a fifty-three-year-old entrepreneur who had been behind a desk or on an airplane for more than thirty years. I signed up for a two-week kayaking trip with eight strangers on the Sea of Cortez in the Gulf of Mexico. The trip was exactly what I needed. Two hours after I checked into NOLS in Mexico, I was in a single-man kayak, hanging upside down underwater, as I practiced a recovery roll in case I capsized in the Sea of Cortez. After spending two weeks with my eight fellow adventurers, sleeping in pup tents, cooking over campfires, and socializing with adult whales and their offspring, I was revitalized. At that time in my life, it was the perfect trip for me.

I recommend this type of trip, especially after a significant change in your life. Going back to nature and immersing yourself in our natural environment is as therapeutic as it gets. My NOLS trip established a degree of confidence in my own physical self-sufficiency, which was particularly beneficial after relying on the commercial self-sufficiency that had been my life for the past thirty years.

When I left for the NOLS trip, I didn't know what I was going to do when I returned. I did know that I still had a lot of energy and I wanted to find a productive way to spend the rest of my working days. I wanted to use the experience that I had gained along my entrepreneurial journey. While on the trip, I recalled a promise I had made to myself almost forty-five years earlier. As a child, my family and I made frequent trips from Washington to New York, where most of our extended family lived. We would emerge from the Tunnel into the Bowery District of New York. Even at that time, it was a poverty-stricken area. On many occasions, I saw the signs of extreme poverty on the streets and in the doorways of this dilapidated neighborhood. When I was eight, I promised myself that I'd find a way to help others if the chance were given to me. The commitment matured into a desire to help those who didn't have the same opportunities that I had and do what I could to raise their standard of living.

I used odd moments under the Mexican sky to begin to plan how I might fulfill that commitment to help people. At the time, I lived about twenty-five miles from Baltimore, a desperately impoverished city. I decided I'd develop a consulting practice to support entrepreneurs and venture capitalists that were starting or expanding their businesses. I'd commit one-third of my waking hours to Lynda and our family, one-third to my consulting business, and one-third to helping emerging victims of poverty. I felt relieved and happy. I had the outline of my life's plan for the next decade, thanks to the therapeutic benefits of my NOLS trip.

Seventeen years later, my ideas have been carried out pretty much as I had planned, except for one major, untimely, and hugely tragic event. It occurred while Lynda, I, and one of our grandchildren were on vacation in northern England in 1992. We were involved in a head-on collision with a semitrailer truck on a rainy, foggy highway. The three of us were critically injured. Our prognosis was grim. The doctors were not sure if we would survive. Over the next seven days, our granddaughter's condition gradually improved. I also recovered, narrowly avoiding the doctors' initial diagnosis that I'd need to have my leg amputated. But Lynda, my partner of thirty-four years, best buddy, and mother of our six children, didn't survive.

It took me more than a year of gut-wrenching anguish to even partially recover from this incident. By far, it was the most difficult experience of my entire life. About six months after the accident, still encased in an external fixture so my leg would heal correctly, Father John Mudd, a friend of ours whom I had known for more than thirty-five years, came to visit. His empathy was clear as he told me that he could understand why I might want to spend the rest of my life in bed. But he counseled me that he didn't think this was what his hero, Jesus Christ, would do. Father John argued persuasively that I had a lot to give to others because of my life's experiences. I remember that day as if it were yesterday. The next Sunday, when the children and grandchildren were visiting, I looked at them and thought to myself that Father John was right. I needed to get up and get going for many reasons, but one of the foremost was my love and respect for all Lynda had done for all of us.

I formed Entrepreneurial Advocates, Inc. (EAI), an organization dedicated to intellectually supporting the successful development of one of America's greatest assets, that is, its entrepreneurs, through consulting. I have now coached more than twenty entrepreneurial companies, mostly in the world of high technology. We developed a plan to found a 501(c) (3) nonprofit organization, which we would name the Entrepreneurial Partnership of Greater Washington (www.epgw.org). This organization performs much the same work as EAI does, but it focuses on America's emerging victims of poverty, drug addiction, and incarceration.

The very best thing that has happen to me since Lynda's death was meeting, courting, and marrying Theresa Cain Hilliard, a mother of three whose husband, John, had tragically died of a brain tumor in 1991 after they had been married for twenty-six years. Terri and I have now lived happily together for fourteen years, and we look forward to many more. As of this writing in 2007, we have nine children and twenty-two grandchildren. Amazingly, neither Terri nor I have ever given up even a scintilla of love for our late spouses, but we love each other to the fullest. God is good!

I'm asked frequently if I'd do it all over again, knowing what I know now. There is no simple answer to this question. When I evaluate my journey in terms of excitement, wealth, challenge, and pride of accomplishment, I know it's something I'd do again in a heartbeat. Still, there are certain considerations that I know now, in retrospect, should be carefully weighed, including:

- **Cash flow problems:** At CES, we never totally missed a payroll. However, during the early days, management was often only receiving partial pay.

- **Major setbacks:** Only once did CES have to make a major reduction in force. Letting 75 percent of the company go was awful, but it was the only road to recovery for CES at that time.

- **Inability to grow with the company:** During my early years, I was so busy hiring for the moment that I failed to ask if the person I was hiring could grow to handle ten times the current demands of the job. This oversight caused me a lot of pain. I had to replace basically good people who were well-intentioned, but they couldn't step up to the next level as CES grew.

- **24-7 commitment:** Entrepreneurial companies, by their nature, are extremely demanding on you, your family, and your friends.

- **Persistence:** Only through not giving up, an entrepreneur can make mistakes and missteps and then use them to do a better job the next time. Entrepreneurs must be relentless.

If I were to do it all again, I'd find an experienced mentor/coach, that is, someone who could be at my side, especially in the early days, to guide me because he had taken an entrepreneurial journey similar to the one that I was contemplating. I can say unequivocally, though, that my experience as an entrepreneur was worth it for me in many ways that I could not have imagined when we began this journey, that is, on the day we brought

Karin home from the hospital in 1964. I hope my story inspires you to shoot for the stars on your own unique entrepreneurial journey.

Appendix A

The Best of the Lessons That I Learned

- Entrepreneurship is a 24-7 job that requires commitment, attitude, planning, and persistence.

- You must have a passion for what you are doing. It's up to you to develop that passion!

- If you knock on enough doors, at least a few will open.

- Constructive dissension is an essential operational tool for any entrepreneurial journey.

- If you can survive, you can thrive.

- Failure is an opportunity to do something over, except you have the benefit of the first experience in hand.

- Whatever you can do or dream you can do, begin it now.

- Acknowledge your mistakes, apologize, fix the problems, and move on.

- A successful entrepreneur must maximize the contributions of each team member.

- An entrepreneur must have alternative courses of action for achieving his or her goals.

- Cash is king of the entrepreneurial kingdom. Whoever holds the cash has the power.

- Everyone needs someone to love, something to do, and something to look forward to. Find them!

- The devil is always in the doing. Get on with it!

- Always hope for the best, but plan for the worst.

- You must have a clearly defined, persuasively presented product or service differentiator in order to succeed. Develop one.

- Timing isn't everything, but it's almost everything. Carefully study the timing of your entry.

- The stock market is obsessed with growth in everything. Ignore this fact at your own peril.

- Every problem should be viewed as an opportunity.

- It's important to know your own and your company's limits. Study them!

- Entrepreneurs must be able to recognize when it's time to move on.

- Never, ever give up!

- A failure to plan is a plan to fail.

- Commit your organization to periodic renewal in order to prevent paralysis.

- Go to associates' strengths and avoid their weaknesses.

Appendix B

Constructive Dissension

In 1969, right after CES received its first financing, I began the process of building an organization that I hoped would become a bright star within the data entry industry. Because my dream was that CES be a really great organization, we sought the "best of the best" associates that we could find. After conducting many interviews with several new team members, we offered the successful candidates lateral entry salaries, complemented with ownership through five-year stock options to be sure they really wanted to join us.

Bringing such a qualified group of engineers, marketing, sales, production, accounting, and administrative stars together kindled its own set of problems. While each associate was a superlative performer in his own discipline, that didn't mean that he or she was particularly tolerant of his colleagues.

At first, I really didn't have a clue on how to handle personality problems. Eventually, we developed a process that we called constructive dissension, which allows all parties with vested interests in any particular issue, event, or program to vent their feelings in an unrestricted meeting environment. We only prohibited personal attacks, which would be a cause for the offending party to leave the meeting. The details of the constructive dissension process are best described in an essay that Steve Kivinski, a writer for the *Baltimore Sun*, and I collaborated on several years ago.

The Value of Constructive Dissension in a Corporate Environment

by

Brian T. Cunningham and Steven S. Kivinski

*Constructive—serving to improve or advance; Dissension—
difference of opinion, disagreement*

Successful corporate and entrepreneurial leaders are intelligent, charismatic, persistent, and disciplined individuals. They succeed by taking charge and leading their organization to ever-higher levels of performance. To maintain continued improvement, an additional skill corporate leaders need is the ability to make effective use of constructive dissension at meetings of executives, management, and employees. At such meetings, the leader takes on the added role of referee and as such is responsible for stimulating the discussion by challenging each participant's contribution with the goal of reaching a better result than would otherwise be achieved. The referee is also responsible for ensuring that the ground rules are abided by and that each participant enters actively into the discussion. In constructive dissension, rather than being a director, the leader becomes a facilitator, orchestrating an in-depth and lively discussion.

Note: The constructive dissension process described herein does not mean that the leader is abdicating his or her authority to committee rule but rather that he or she is using the constructive forum to evoke a higher degree of intellectual focus on a given problem. The leader then must pick and choose from what he or she knows to be the strengths and weakness of their constituency, which opinions he or she will listen to or discount.

Experience has shown that the use of constructive dissension simultaneously raises the level and increases the depth of the discussion. Through the challenging of ideas presented, participants are encouraged to "push the envelope" of their own thinking and that of their colleagues. This type of meeting provides a venue where colleagues feel safe to disagree with and challenge one another. The result for the company is a better solution to the problem than could have been arrived at by the CEO alone or in one-on-one discussions. Furthermore, those who take part in the constructive dissension discussion are now invested in solving the problem successfully.

Scientists and engineers have long subscribed to the concept of constructive dissension as a means of promoting advancements in their field of study. In academia, discord is used to help generate creativity, independent thinking, and new ideas. The decision-making process is enhanced by the exchange of ideas and opinions. Senior corporate executives need to learn the art of constructive dissension as a means of advancing the company's ability to function as a team, fostering new and different ideas and maximizing the talents of its associates and the success of the company. In *Winning Decisions: Getting It Right the First Time*, coauthor J. Edward Russo states that effective leaders not only encourage discussion, debate, and deliberation but also intentionally surround themselves with dissimilar teammates.

Good leaders select, tolerate, respect, and reward people with diverse opinion.
They thank people with different opinions even when they disagree. Strong
leaders can accept that dissension. Weak leaders can't.

As movers and shakers in the business world, it is crucial for corporate leaders to be open to investigating and accepting differences especially within the community of their own company. However, management needs to find ways to enable employees to contribute. By creating an environment that encourages constructive debate, management taps into the competencies in each of the various departments (i.e., marketing, engineering, operations) that will give the company a competitive advantage. Constructive dissension brings to light the different ideas that executives and employees have based on their differing backgrounds and experience, and it is these very differences that need to be encouraged and utilized in reaching solutions to problems.

A Constructive Dissension Meeting

Preparation is essential for a constructive dissension meeting. Prior to the meeting, the leader/CEO must provide all participants with a meeting agenda memorandum. The memorandum should include the following:

- The subject matter of the meeting presented in a stimulating way

- A directive to all participants to think of pertinent questions prior to the meeting

- The expectation that all attendees will participate proactively

- The leader will challenge all ideas presented in order to reach the best possible solution.

- Participants are invited to challenge each other's proposals and suggestions.

- All opinions are to be respected, regardless of professional background.

- Personal statements about or attacks on another participant will not be tolerated.

- Following the meeting, the CEO will prepare a statement of conclusions to be presented to participants for their review and comment.

- A critical agenda will be produced that defines the job to be done, individual responsibilities, and a timeline.

The success of the meeting depends on the ability of the leader/referee and on the mix of participants. Some people are naturally challenging and skeptical, while others rarely question the status quo. For the discussion, a leader needs to include those who are willing to topple old ideas and who believe in change passionately enough to make it happen. Research shows that for economic and psychological security, most employees want to be accepted and are predisposed to agree with their boss and their colleagues. However, a properly conducted constructive dissension meeting can overcome this tendency by providing a place where opposing views can be safely expressed.

The makeup of the group can vary, according to what is appropriate. Some meetings will involve only senior people, such as the CEO, COO, CFO, CIO, HRO, et cetera. Others will be comprised of managers of departments or of members of one department only. Once the participants have been chosen, the leader must provide them with the meeting's objective, agenda, and the topics to be discussed and distribute this to the participants in a timely manner.

The leader/referee needs to immediately impart a sense of energy and commitment to the task, affirming that the goal is to find the best solution for the benefit of the organization. The leader's attitude and enthusiasm will determine the attitude and enthusiasm of the participants. To reach the best solution, the leader and others are encouraged to identify root causes rather than just symptoms of problems. What each participant says will be tested but such testing must be constructive.

There must be an acceptance among all participants that views and opinions will differ and that this contributes to the ultimate solution. There are no bad or dumb ideas in a brainstorming session of this type. The leader must ensure that the group examines each proposal from every conceivable perspective and does not shrug off any dissenting opinions. The leader should ensure that each proposal regardless of merit is responded to. If appropriate, the group can be divided into smaller groups to discuss specific topics with each group having its own referee. The leader should remind participants that constructive debate and the introduction of alternative ideas in formulating company decisions are positive and healthy signs of involvement in the company.

In the statement of conclusions and critical agenda to be produced by the leader/CEO after the meeting, each person's commitment will be spelled out with the clear understanding that such commitments must be met. The timeline must be adhered to and each participant must keep the group apprised of progress. Any changes to the original agenda and timeline will be negotiated with the group.

Conclusion

People are empowered when they are given security combined with freedom and opportunity: the security of knowing they will be heard in a safe environment and have the support of management; the freedom to accomplish using creativity and initiative; and the opportunity to bring new ideas and concepts to enhance the success of the organization. Constructive dissension is one of the best tools available to corporations for creating an environment of security, freedom, and opportunity for its management and employees. Encouraging dissension that leads to lively and constructive discussions enables new ideas and innovations to surface that might otherwise have remained dormant.

Constructive dissension meetings help to break down barriers to communication, especially between associates and management. Such meetings empower teamwork, maximize the use of human resources, and increase productivity. Constructive dissension can be seen as the incubator for new ideas and a means to create a stronger team capable of integrating discipline, knowledge, and experience.

As noted at the beginning of this abstract, an entrepreneurial/corporate leader is usually able to inspire and lead successfully on his or her own at the beginning, but if the company is to grow and succeed for the long term, learning the art of constructive dissension puts another all-important skill in the leader's hands so that the company's future is built on the very best ideas generated from throughout the company through the process of constructive dissension.

Bibliography

Gebelein, Stevens, Skube, Lee, Davis, and Heldervik. *Successful Manager's Handbook: Development Suggestions for Today's Managers.* Personnel Decisions International Corporation, 2000.

Maxwell, John C. *Developing the Leaders Around You: How to Help Others Reach Their Full Potential.* Thomas Welson Publishers, 1993.

Micale, Frances A. *Not Another Meeting! A Practical Guide for Facilitating Effective Meetings.* The Oasis Press, 1999.

Prendergast, Candice. 1993. A Theory of 'Yes Men.' *American Economic Review.*

Rasiel, Ethan M. *The McKinsey Way, Using the Techniques of the World's Top Strategic Consultants to Help You and Your Business.* McGraw-Hill, 1999.

Russo, J. Edward. *Winning Decisions: Getting It Right the First Time.* Harbor Press Inc., 2001.

Wheatley, Margaret J. *Leading for Innovation and Organizing for Results: The Drucker Foundation.* Jossey-Bass, 2001.

Summary

- Properly organized, constructive dissension is a tool that management can use to create differentiators for its company that can keep it ahead of competition.

- The process of constructive dissension can become leveraged when organizers proactively seek to bring in colleagues with differing cultures, genders, and professional backgrounds.

- Sometimes, the quietest one in the room can make the biggest contribution. It is up to the organizer to get all attendees to actively participate.

- Constructive dissension meetings should be free-for-alls; however, personal attacks cannot be part of the landscape and should not be tolerated, so that participants can feel comfortable in presenting their dissension views.

Questions

1. How should you choose your future constructive dissension team?

2. List at least three characteristics for each person on your team that you think have added value to you and your team.

3. List the characteristics that have negatively affected the constructive dissension process.

4. What are the important lessons you have learned from practicing constructive dissension today?

Appendix C

Chapter Summaries and Questions

One of the driving forces behind the preparation of Never Give Up! *was the need to bring a sampling of entrepreneurial reality to EPGW's (see Chapter 18 for a description of EPGW) developing entrepreneurs by engaging them in the processes of Constructive Dissension (see Appendix B) during the term of EPGW's Course. The summaries and questions that follow represent my answer to this challenge.*

Chapter One: Climbing the Corporate Ladder
Summary

- Passion is defined as Commitment, Attitude, Planning, and Persistence (CAPP) and is an essential ingredient to a successful entrepreneurial journey. Measure each of these vital building blocks, one at a time, against your physical, intellectual, emotional, and spiritual willingness on a scale of 0–10 to extract your passion for your entrepreneurial journey.

- Timing isn't everything, but it's almost everything. Use this observation in your planning.

- A supportive family is an essential part of your entrepreneurial journey. It isn't always what you know. It is also who you know that can win the day. Cultivate relationships.

- When opportunity knocks, don't leap at the opportunity but do leap to the planning, after which, you can decide to leap at the opportunity.

- When you are raising capital, know both the rules and the players. Be prepared to make great sacrifice to provide the return you promise.

- To thine own self, above all else, always be true.

- Adapt, adapt, and adapt some more.

Questions

1. What does it take to be an entrepreneur? What challenges do you anticipate on your entrepreneurial journey?

2. Why do you want to be an entrepreneur?

3. What is fear to you? Recall a situation where you have faced fear and its outcome.

4. How do you handle interpersonal conflicts with your colleagues? Suggest some resolution techniques that you have used to address disputes between your business and personal lives.

Chapter Two: On the Road Again
Activities

You are forming a new company. You are planning the management structure you would like to establish and maintain at your new company. Analyze the advantages and disadvantages of a centralized ad hoc pyramid management structure with the top-down decision-making process versus a decentralized management structure. What are some of the pros and cons of each method? Which type of organizational structure is more likely to support the constructive dissension process?

The following are brief job descriptions for those who might be involved in a constructive dissension meeting. Assemble into groups of five. Each group member can select a position from the following list for fifteen minutes of constructive dissension. Practice constructive dissension on any subject, according to the outline provided. At least twice during the session, alternate the roles of participants.

Chief Executive Officer	• Reports to the board of directors
	• Responsible for the overall success or failure of the venture, including sales and profit growth, corporate image, new product/market development and, most importantly, the well-being of all associates and stockholders
	• Only person to have the authority and responsibility to direct the new company to a successful future
Vice President of Sales	• Reports to the CEO
	• Responsible for hiring a sales force to create sufficient company backlog in a timely manner at corporately mandated prices to ensure integrity of the company going forward
Vice President of R&D	• Reports to the CEO
	• Responsible for timely, cost-effective, reliable, and when possible, patentable product designs based on recommendations made by the marketing department and approved by the CEO
Vice President of Finance	• Reports to CEO
	• Responsible for the financial management of the company, including budgets, cash flow, debt and equity funding, controlling expenses, and the overall financial welfare of the organization
Vice President of Marketing	• Reports to the CEO
	• Responsible for the company's image which strongly influences a customer's decision and should be established prior to the first sales call, so as to set the right mood for the sale

---

- Responsible for the development of new or expanding markets to provide the company in general and the sales force in particular with proposals for unique, differentiated, cost-effective, and otherwise attractive products and services to secure the company objectives of growth and success

---

Chapter Three: Failure Is an Opportunity in Disguise
Summary

- If you can adjust to the circumstances, failure presents opportunity.

- When things aren't going right after a proper trial period, change the paradigm by taking action through education and change in your actions and/or behavior.

- Always take CLARE with you on any relationship-building effort.

- To be successful, find a successful role model. Copy within the bounds of morality. Then commit to improve the model through R&D.

Activities

1. What would enable you to become a more successful salesperson? What is your most successful approach to engaging a potential customer?

2. Describe your favorite sales stories (successful and unsuccessful).

3. Why was the sale not successful? How can you correct the failure?

4. What is your view of failure in life, in a business venture, or on a sales appointment?

5. Describe one situation in which you failed. How did you eventually overcome or how do you think that you might overcome your failure?

6. Write a brief description of one personal circumstance where you failed. How were you able to overcome the failure?

7. Describe the most important characteristic that helped you overcome this failure.

8. Name the areas in your business that you haven't been as successful as you would like to be. Define the action(s) required to fix each area.

9. List the ways you can overcome this failure to make it an opportunity.

Practice #1

Failure is a commonplace event for individuals in start-up companies. Understanding failures' impact on the company and the team is vital to your future success. Assemble a constructive dissension group consisting of a sales manager and two to three sales representatives. The person acting as the sales manager takes the lead in organizing a constructive dissension meeting with the sales force. Use the following questions to help stimulate discussion. Go around the group so that everyone participates.

- Describe your favorite approach for engaging a potential customer.

- What is your favorite war story of a successful sale?

- What is your worst sales nightmare? How would you bail yourself out?

- What can management do to best support you in terms of increasing sales?

- Is your company organized well enough for you to do the best possible job at selling its products? Why is the answer yes or no?

- Do you have sufficient authority to accomplish your job?

- Are your responsibilities clearly defined?

- What is the biggest problem you face in your day-to-day job?

- What would your dream work request be?

- Where do you want to be, professionally and personally, five and ten years from now?

Practice #2

Partner up with another person to make a team that consists of a salesperson and a customer. Perform the following activities:

- Pick any product visible in the room and sell it to your partner.

- Practice the CLARE approach.

- Demonstrate your sales technique in front of the class.

- Evaluate the other's performance.

Chapter Four: Commitment
Summary

- Commitment, attitude, planning, and persistence (CAPP), as measured in each case by the entrepreneur's physical, intellectual, emotional, and spiritual feelings about the undertaking, become the underlying reasons for its success.

- Create and recognize your own internal passion for the success of yourself and your company.

- Seek out and nourish a relationship with a competent, patient person who is willing to counsel you in the development of your company's project plans.

- Sometimes, it is better to lose a battle in order to win a war.

Activities

"Every problem or inconvenience is a potential opportunity to create something new." Assume that you have an idea for a new company, a seafood franchise that does catering and fast food. You and others believe you have met the value-proposition test. You see yourself as either the leader or a strong contributor to the business over the next five to fifteen years. You have assembled a team of constructive dissenters. You hope many may later join the new company at some later date. You take the lead at the meeting by asking each participant to answer the following questions:

1. What does commitment mean to you? Define commitment in your own words.

2. For your business, what does it take to be committed? List the factors, discuss with your colleagues, and create a master list of what you think that it takes to be committed.

3. Because the success of a business is determined primarily by the people who run it, what role do you see yourself having in the new venture? Why?

4. What are your biggest concerns about your business idea?

5. In your own words, define what commitment means. Tell how committed you are to the success of the new company.

6. Assuming the new company is able to meet your salary requirements, what time duration (years) are you willing to commit to the company?

7. What are your thoughts on corporate ownership, profit sharing, and management participation (ownership) for yourself and the new company as a whole?

8. What role does the business plan play in deepening your commitment to the venture?

9. Do you believe that, if the new company survives, it will thrive? If so, how can you improve the opportunity and accelerate its success?

10. What do you see as your personal growth potential? Where do you think you might top out? Share a situation/time in your life where your commitment has brought fruitful results.

Chapter Five: A Board for All Seasons
Summary

- The organization and staffing of the company's board of directors is a vitally important function of the company's chairman and CEO. They should work closely together to develop the best board possible.

- Board members are usually very busy people. For them to be effective, it's your job to keep them well informed about, interested in, and enthusiastic about your company.

- Define your expectations carefully before recruiting board members. Then take your time in assessing their abilities to contribute.

- Term limits on board tenure offer a comfortable exit for either party, assuming such is required.

Activities

Complete the following chart for your current company or for your planned company.

	Member 1	Member 2	Member 3	Member 4
Specific Relevant Experience of Office				
Oversight Responsibility				
Team Player				
Specific Responsibilities				

Questions

1. What are the most important lessons you learned on how to form a board?

2. What are some of the mistakes you would like to avoid in forming your company's board?

3. List the set of people you would consider for a board you are going to form.

4. Write down three strengths and three potential weaknesses for each one of these candidates.

5. For each member you are considering for your board, discuss their characteristics with your peers.

6. What challenges are you facing in forming the board of directors for your company?

Chapter Six: Creating the Necessary Alternatives
Summary

- You and your team should proactively undertake the development of reasonable and creative alternative solutions to corporate problems.

- Verifiable customer testimonials, provided by active and reputable users, can add substantial credibility to the entrepreneurial offering.

- Sometimes, even the most well-intentioned client needs a little push to close an agreement. It is up to the entrepreneur to find a way to make this happen.

- It never hurts to take a little bit of profit along the way. It is good for the soul and good for the family.

Activities
Practice #1

Use constructive dissension and what you have learned in this chapter to describe how you and your team would handle the following situation. You are the leader of a new company. You have developed and vetted a business plan that will employ five to ten associates and do $1 million in revenues at 10 percent profit after taxes. You need $50,000 for equipment, facilities, salaries, and overhead to get to where the company can show sufficient progress to warrant a larger investment. Engage your team in discussion on the following:

1. How will the new company make the best possible presentation of its plan?

2. Who will the new company make its presentations to?

3. Who will make the presentations? Who is considered best able to persuade investors to fund the company?

4. What progress can the new company make with its plan while waiting for funding?

5. Does anyone know of a larger, financially successful business that might join with the new company with an opportunity to buy you once you are successful?

6. Because the leader will play a major role in fund-raising, the new company needs a CEO who will organize a sales department in order to establish the validity of the new company's products and services with investors. Who wants to be sales manager? Why are you equipped to perform the job?

7. While we are fund-raising, how do we keep all those involved in the new company informed of our progress?

8. Does anyone have additional ideas of how to obtain the funding we need?

Practice #2

"The development of alternatives should be a primary reason for writing the business plan."

1. What are some industries that have recently experienced a downturn or economic difficulties? Analyze the industry's internal and external environments. Propose a strategy for your company to solve the problem.

2. Provide a plan of action.

Practice #3

For your current or planned business, outline at least three scenarios with contingency plans and alternatives.

Scenario	Outcome: if things go as planned	Outcome: if things do not go as planned	Alternatives	Expected Alternative Results

Chapter Seven: Persistence
Summary

*   I hope you see the benefit of having alternatives. If CES hadn't begun the development of OCR upon receiving its capital infusion from Company X, CES probably would have never survived.

*   I have always taught, "To thine own self be true." But I failed to follow my own advice by not insisting on performance indicators for Company X. I paid the price for this oversight.

*   The timing of Entron's demise and the ascension of CES, as well as our ability to take advantage of this opportunity, was instrumental in the ultimate success of CES.

*   Even though well-intentioned professionals worked at CES and Company X, the culture and environmental conditions in each company meant they were worlds apart.

Activities
Practice #1

The new company, of which you are chairman and CEO, has just lost the biggest contract it has ever had. It has to figure out what to do now. Your job is to conduct a constructive dissension meeting to discuss:

1. What new business should the new company be in?

2. What people resources does the new business require?

3. How and when does the new company downsize to adjust for your contract loss?

4. Who will tell the staff about the contract loss? When?

5. What can the new company do for those who are being laid off?

6. Are there any other alternatives?

7. What can you do to prevent this situation from happening again?

8. What could or should you have done differently to avoid the contract loss?

9. How does a successful company succeed?

10. What motivates the successful person to continue to pursue his or her dream?

11. In your business, have you encountered any unsuccessful experiences? Evaluate how you reacted to them. Describe how you would react now.

12. Laying off people is an extremely difficult task. What would you suggest is the best way to approach the issue? Are there any other alternatives when it comes to cutting costs?

Practice #2

Discuss a business leader who you most admired for his or her persistence and his or her success stories.

Practice #3

Examine your experience. Share your story of persistence.

1. List some of the worst times that you have been through in business and personal life.

2. What were some of the reasons why you were able to get through those situations?

3. Was persistence one of those reasons?

Chapter Eight: Shooting for the Stars
Summary

*   When in doubt, after a careful review, shoot for the stars. You may hit the moon.

*   A fresh plan prepared in a group setting will serve to promote commitment, healthy attitudes, effective planning, and corporate persistence (CAPP).

*   Always take an inventory of your assets and liabilities before committing to a new plan of action.

*   Take aggressive advantage of every opportunity coming your way.

*   The essential components of an entrepreneur's toolbox are something to do, someone to love, and something to look forward to.

Activities

1. What is the most important thing you learned from this chapter?

2. What are your dreams?

3. How are you going to effectively shoot for your stars? What are the steps? What is your plan of action?

4. Describe your company's niche market opportunity, technical expertise/leadership, resources, industry environment, and marketing and selling ability required.

Chapter Nine: Finally, Breaking Even!
Summary

- There are many ways to solve problems, but you have to find the one that fits your style. Then, work it!

- Like small corporations, big corporations usually have good moral values, but you may have to look a little further in the big company. Start at the top!

- It isn't necessarily what you know. It is who you know that can make a big difference. Cultivate relationships!

- When you find a person worth supporting, find a way to support him or her, at all costs.

- Truthfully and carefully crafted, the written word has much greater value and can be distributed to a much larger audience than the spoken word.

- It never hurts to ask customers to help finance the production of products that they will benefit from, particularly when the product is unique.

Questions

1. What are your personal and professional reactions to the events described in this chapter?

2. What might you have done differently?

3. Could the CES eviction have been avoided? If so, how?

4. What are your opinions about corporate America as they relate to this incident? Has Pfizer's turnaround changed your views? If so, how?

Chapter Ten: Have Check, Will Travel
Summary

- It's always best to check your credit before engaging in a somewhat irreversible transaction.

- If there's a will, there is usually a way. Keep on probing for the way.

- Don't count yourself out too early!

Questions

1. What lessons can you glean from the author's experiences at the tire dealership?

2. How would you have solved the payment problem with the Michelin dealer?

Chapter Eleven: Where Do We Go From Here?
Summary

- Where there is great risk, there can be great gain. Under these conditions, it is essential to carefully study all of your company's options over prolonged sessions of constructive dissension.

- Large, highly organized companies tend to become bureaucratic. If you are able to recognize the signs, it can become a competitive advantage for a fast-moving entrepreneurial company.

- Timing can't be controlled, but you can take advantage of it.

- Keep in touch with your strengths and weaknesses as you move forward. In retrospect, it would have been a disaster if CES had tried to go public in the early seventies. By the early eighties, it was much better equipped to adjust to the rigors of running a company.

- Where there is great risk, there can be great gain. Measure your situation carefully. Then take action!

Questions

1. Given the facts cited in this chapter, what do you think your decision as a CES board member would have been, relative to voting for an IPO?

2. Is the precipitous nature of the 1980 decision clear to you? Why?

3. If you had been a CES board member, what alternative might you have come up with for another course of action?

4. What benefit(s) do you perceive that CES's investors, board, and associates derive from the decision to go public?

5. From your perspective, is the reward at this juncture in the story worth the pain of the twelve years that CES had undergone since it was founded?

6. What are your thoughts and reactions on this chapter's events?

7. Describe the advantages and disadvantages of CES's decision to go public. What might you have done differently?

8. Describe why you would or wouldn't like to run a private or public company.

Chapter Twelve: Corporate Renewal: Luxury or Necessity?
Summary

- Given the ways of man and corporate life, if you don't take steps to renew yourself regularly, your company will probably lose its edge.

- Everyone likes to feel as if he or she is very much a part of something bigger than he or she is. The meeting agenda presents an ideal opportunity for corporate leadership to shine by involving corporate doers in the process.

- If your proactive endeavors can encourage associates to perform 10 percent better than competition, you have achieved your objective.

- Stay close to your associates and your customers. The rewards can be compelling.

Questions

1. What are the signs that you might look for in your organization to determine that it is time for a corporate retreat?

2. What are the benefits that you think your organization might derive from a corporate retreat?

3. Who would you invite to such a retreat?

4. What are the potential negatives, if any, of such a retreat?

Chapter Thirteen: Becoming and Running a Public Company Summary

- Going public is a major decision within your corporate life. Be sure you have the right people in the right positions in your company before you take this big step.

- Do the best you can to ensure that the next year or two of your company's financial performance is well-assured. The stock market can be very unforgiving for new entries that fail to meet expectations.

- Carefully reflect on the fact that everything by design becomes known to the public, including your customers, during the process of the offering. Get ready for any skeletons in the closet to emerge.

- Be sure that the value proposition comes down on the positive side for you and your company before subjecting yourself to the rigors of running a public company.

Activities

Constructively discuss the most recent IPOs and the pros and cons of becoming a public company.

1. Does your company have a suitable differentiator to excite the public's interest?

2. How big is the market you are attacking? Assuming success, is it large enough to satisfy your company's growth objectives?

3. Is your market growing?

4. What financial resources do you require to achieve your corporate objectives?

5. What skills will be needed?

6. What is the time frame?

7. How do you define success in terms of sales and profits growth and return on investment?

Questions

1. What are some effects an IPO can have on the company, management, employees, and shareholders?

2. What are some opportunities and problems that present themselves after an IPO? How would you tackle the problems?

Chapter Fourteen: I Wasn't Careful Enough!
Summary

- You can't be careful enough. However, when unforeseen problems develop, an entrepreneur and his team should never ever give up!

- Things can get better because of unforeseen reasons, but you have to stay in the game to benefit from these opportunities.

- Check, recheck, and then double-check references prior to making a corporate move that is of vital consequence to your organization.

Questions

1. What would you do if you hired someone who misrepresented himself?

2. To what degree would you be embarrassed by the events that occurred between Mr. E and CES?

Chapter Fifteen: Growth through Mergers
Summary

- Creation of a mutually acceptable PMOP by the operating management of both organizations is the single most important step that can be taken in an effort to assure the merger's success.

- Mergers are difficult. Essentially, they represent the combination of two independently developed cultures. It takes a lot of work on the part of both organizations to achieve the new culture that the buyer desires.

- Stay close to your associates and the customers to feel the pulse of the transaction.

- Quickly make senior management appearances before the new customer base as soon as a deal is announced.

- As soon as an announcement is possible, go to excessive lengths to welcome and present your company's philosophies and reward system(s).

Questions

1. Which type of growth, organic or inorganic, is more appealing to you? Why?

2. If you had been a member of the CES board, how would you have voted on the issue of taking the company public? What alternative strategies/tactics might you have suggested to mitigate some of the risks mentioned?

3. What would be your major/minor concerns about running a public or private company?

Chapter Sixteen: The Sale of CES
Summary

- Everything and every company have a time and place. It is your job as the CEO to sense the timing of the market life of your company and its products.

- Spend time on computing your own and your company's thresholds.

Questions

1. What are your thoughts on equipping your company for orders of magnitude in growth?

2. Considering CES's growth over twenty years from $0 to $77 million in revenues and sixteen consecutive years of profitability, how would you vote relative to sale of the company? Why?

3. What alternatives might you have offered to the sale of the company?

4. Given the company's success and proven management team, did a premature sale of CES shortchange shareholders?

5. What do you think the negatives were to selling the company?

Chapter Seventeen: Ideal Characteristics of the Entrepreneurial Leader
Summary

- For the most part, successful entrepreneurs are not genetically dependent. But they develop themselves through years of hard work, both in the classroom and on the job.

- If there is a will, there is a way. Persistence must be the driving force.

- Timing is almost everything. After careful consideration, including multiple constructive dissension sessions, CES's board voted to sell.

Questions

1. How do you rank "out of the box" as an entrepreneur? Are you willing to make a ten hour/week commitment to work on characteristics that need further development?

2. Do you have a role model entrepreneur whom you can study and emulate?

3. Which of the suggested characteristics concerns you the most? How will you address it?

Chapter Eighteen: What Will I Do Now?
Summary

- Life is really just one big challenge after another. Learn to enjoy it!

- Doing things for others who are having a difficult time can be more rewarding than corporate achievements.

- Getting back to nature is a great rejuvenator for a tired executive looking for physical, intellectual, and emotional renewal. Take a break!

- As you plan your company's or your own future, try and do it in ten-year incremental goals. This will give you enough time to really accomplish something that you can be proud of.

Questions

1. What are your thoughts regarding spending time in nature to reinvigorate yourself? What would you do?

2. What do you think about giving entrepreneurship a try?

3. What are your biggest fears with regard to such a journey?

7600 System—The 7600 System is used primarily by the banking industry for the rehabilitation and processing of rejected checks which are not readable by normal magnetic scanning devices.

7100 System—The 7100 System is used principally in check and monthly bill processing, loan payment processing, inventory control and insurance premium processing.

7050 System—The 7050 System is a hand fed system used for receipt processing of credit card charge slips and is primarily intended for use by credit card firms, bank card associations and oil companies.

The CES product line consists of modular, microprocessor based, electro-mechanical optical character reader systems which are used to reduce data processing labor expense and expedite funds collection in the banking, retail, insurance and utility industries.

NEW ISSUE

700,000 Shares

Computer Entry Systems Corporation

COMMON STOCK

Price $7.00 Per Share

Copies of the Prospectus may be obtained from any of the several Underwriters only in such states in which such Underwriters are qualified to act as dealers in securities and in which the Prospectus may be legally distributed.

Hambrecht & Quist   Baker, Watts & Co.

Allen & Company   Bear, Stearns & Co.   L. F. Rothschild, Unterberg, Towbin
Incorporated
Arnhold and S. Bleichroeder, Inc.   Basle Securities Corporation   Casenove Inc.

F. Eberstadt & Co., Inc.   Robert Fleming   Ladenburg, Thalmann & Co. Inc.
Incorporated
New Court Securities Corporation   Tucker, Anthony & R. L. Day, Inc.

Compagnie de Banque et d'Investissements   Credit Commercial de France   Grieveson Grant & Company
(Underwriters) S.A.
Okasan Securities Co., Ltd.   Pictet International Ltd.   Pierson, Heldring & Pierson N.V.

Vereins- und Westbank   Butcher & Singer Inc.   Janney Montgomery Scott Inc.
Aktiengesellschaft
Johnson, Lane, Space, Smith & Co., Inc.   Legg Mason Wood Walker   Neuberger & Berman
Incorporated
Parker/Hunter   The Robinson-Humphrey Company, Inc.   Wheat, First Securities, Inc.
Incorporated
Brean Murray, Foster Securities Inc.   Bruns, Nordeman, Rea & Co.   Cowen & Co.

Interstate Securities Corporation   Johnston, Lemon & Co.   John Muir & Co.
Incorporated
Raymond, James & Associates, Inc.   Branch, Cabell & Co.   Ferris & Company
Incorporated
Galleher & Company, Inc.   Laidlaw Adams & Peck Inc.

April 15, 1981

Afterword

January 2005

David, one of this book's reviewers, lamented, "You left me hanging! What's the rest of the story?"

My first reaction was to say, "Enough is enough!"

Later, I decided I owed it to readers, who have come this far with me on my journey, to tell the rest of the story, as it is now unfolding.

After Lynda, my first true love, died, I was completely devastated. But during the later stages of my physical and emotional recovery from the accident, I determined that after having enjoyed such a great married life with Lynda, I could not make the rest of my life's journey alone. I began to date, and I eventually met Terri. From our very first meeting, probably because of the empathy we had for each other because we had both experienced the death of a spouse, we felt as if we were reborn. I courted Terri for fourteen months, after which she accepted my proposal. We were married in the fall of 1993. I settled into a life of consulting, investing, coaching start-up companies, and investing in the stock market. Terri actively pursued her lifelong love of estate sales and plein oil painting. Life as newlyweds in our fifties was as good as it could be, and we lived our senior years to their fullest.

On the negative side, we did take a financial hit when the stock market, where I had most of my CES winnings, collapsed in 2000. Nonetheless, we continue to enjoy life, although perhaps not in so grand a style as prior to the market collapse. But my life at the age of seventy has taken an unusual, challenging, and potentially rewarding turn. Terri and I formed the EPGW because of our concern for the level of poverty in America. We are proud to say that, over the past eight years, EPGW has successfully developed a replicable curriculum in entrepreneurship. It has graduated fifty-four of the one hundred inner-city entrepreneurs who started our sixteen-week course.

This course is conducted one evening a week, and participants attend a Saturday morning computer class as well. It demands about four to six hours of homework each week. With few exceptions, these potential entrepreneurs have, on average, tenth-grade educations. To pass EPGW's course, they are required, with the aid of enthusiastic volunteers, who are currently enrolled as business majors in college, called entrepreneurial advocates (EAs), to meet the following requirements:

- Within the first two weeks of the first class, prepare a one- to two-page value proposition defining what their business venture will bring to themselves and their communities.

- Prepare a two- to three-page executive summary that provides a five-year overview of their business, including abbreviated financial projections. The executive summary then becomes their business plan outline. It can be used to introduce their venture to investors while a more detailed business plan is being developed over the ninety-day course period. This period provides the time that it takes to consider all of the possible scenarios under any possible circumstances.

- Using a computer-based template, create a forty- to fifty-page five-year business plan, which addresses all aspects of their new venture, including a five-year income, balance sheet, and cash flow statement.

- Prepare and deliver a two-minute pitch on their business, which will be delivered from the stage at graduation ceremonies.

None of this would be possible without our enthusiastic and dedicated volunteer mentors. The EAs are encouraged to help the entrepreneurs as much as possible via e-mail, phone, fax, or private meetings. Most of EPGW's entrepreneurs lack the academic background to write the business plan on their own, but they blend synergistically with the EAs' strengths.

EPGW's governing rule is that the entrepreneurs must be able to prepare and present the final version of their business plans and answer questions on their own. The combination of energetic, compassionate EAs and future entrepreneurs is probably the most satisfying accomplishment that EPGW has achieved to date.

While EPGW has graduated fifty-four entrepreneurs, only fourteen businesses have been started. These young people, who are willing to work very hard, can't raise the required financing to start their businesses. They are not earning a salary, and they do not have the collateral to meet conventional bank-lending standards.

Before we incorporated EPGW, Terri and I knew that conventional banking bylaws and lending practices would probably be an obstacle, but we thought we might be able to appeal to the Small Business Administration or humanitarian foundations. That, however, hasn't worked, at least not to the degree that EPGW desires. Therefore, to reach EPGW's objective of confronting economic and social poverty through entrepreneurship by starting one hundred new businesses in the inner city over the next decade, EPGW found another way to raise the required start-up capital in the form of a revolving loan program, wherein all members of the group guarantee each other's loans. Only in this way can we build a successful entrepreneurship model program, a sound and logical method for confronting poverty.

During EPGW's incubation period, Terri's sister-in-law, Marie, informed us that she and several colleagues would be returning from Ireland via Washington. Marie and her traveling companions had been in Ireland to assist in the mediation of a peace treaty between the English and the Irish, a treaty that I never thought was possible because of the centuries of hatred and bitterness between these two nations.

Marie invited us to what was to become a dinner that would change our course. As coffee was served, one of the senior peace treaty negotiators, a Presbyterian minister, surprised us when he asked that each person in attendance describe what he or she was doing to improve the welfare of less fortunate members of society, either in the United States or overseas.

When Terri's and my turn came, we described the essence of EPGW's mission. Several of the attendees applauded our work and wanted to be kept up to date on our progress.

Next to speak was Bob Conant, a retired thirty-year Dow Chemical chemist, who described a humanitarian project that shook me to the core of my being.

Bob asked a simple question, "Of the six billion people on earth, how many lack water clean enough to drink? How many people die each year from either lack of water or disease-ridden water?"

A few of the dinner attendees, most of whom were well-educated, ventured responses. Each time they did, Bob would point his index finger in an upward direction. Guest estimates quickly rose for those without access to fresh (potable) water from ten million to one hundred million. By the time Bob finally nodded assent, the number was more than one billion. Three million people were dying every year. Half of this number was children.

After that dinner, Terri and I decided we needed to try and be part of the solution to this horrendous problem. Over the next year, we researched solutions related to earth's water supply and discovered a two-hundred-year-old technology called slow sand filtering (SSF), which allows a family to pour contaminated water into a small barrel. Inside the barrel, the contaminated water goes through the sand filter. It is then emitted in a 98 percent purified state. We went to Rubbermaid and got them interested in making the filters. Then we applied to the World Bank for a grant to conduct a battery of tests throughout Africa, where we had developed missionary contacts in remote villages. Unfortunately, because we didn't have any prior relationship with the World Bank, we were turned down on our grant request for reasons that were never made clear.

Meanwhile, as we continued our research on worldwide potable water, the more we found out, the worse the situation sounded. Only about 2 percent of the total water on earth is available for consumption. The rest is either saline water or water so contaminated by bacteria that it's useless.

Perhaps the previous secretary-general of the United Nations, Kofi Annan, provided the most succinct and revealing description of the world's water crisis, *"We shall not finally defeat AIDS, tuberculosis, malaria, or any of the other infectious diseases that plague the developing world until we have also won the battle for safe drinking water, sanitation, and basic health care."[7]*

In June 2004, my high school class celebrated its fiftieth reunion. There, I reconnected with a former classmate, Michael McCormick whom I had not seen or spoken to since the night that we graduated 50 years earlier. In the years since our graduation, Michael had earned the title of Dr. Michael McCormick, holding three PhDs. All of his work is related to the capture of ocean wave energy to desalinate salt water to relieve mankind's scarcity of freshwater. Michael had spent the past twenty-five years in an illustrious career, researching and teaching ocean wave energy at the Naval Academy in Annapolis and Johns Hopkins University in Baltimore. How providential for two high school friends, meeting for the first time in fifty years, to both be interested in, working on, and concerned about the earth's water crisis!

Now, at the age of seventy, I'm taking on a new business challenge. Although it's fraught with many reasons that should dissuade me from going forward, for example, the need for money and major technical challenges among them, I can see the light at the end of the tunnel. And I can never give up!

Michael and I met regularly for the next year to determine how we could join forces to relieve the world's water crisis. I proposed to Michael that we form a new company, which we would name Ocean Energy Systems (OES). The mission of OES would be to design, develop, demonstrate, and distribute ocean wave energy conversion systems for the desalinization of sea water. Michael agreed, stipulating I accept the position of CEO. I leapt at the opportunity.

In the spring of 2005, we incorporated OES. Over the next six months, OES developed its executive summary along with a ninety-six–page business plan describing the following:

• The market

- Our unique product, the Amplified Wave Energy Conversion System (AWECS)

- The details of how OES would bring this product to market for humanitarian reasons as well as the potential of a venture capital return

OES and I are now in the process of seeking funding, much the same as I was doing almost forty years ago. OES requires a total of $25 million–$10 million to demonstrate its proprietary Linear Inductance Generator and potable-water-producing Amplified Wave Energy Conversion System (AWECS) and another $15 million to bring our company to positive cash flow over a five- to-seven-year period. Success, which we will achieve, in this venture will begin the process of bringing both potable water and electricity to the have-nots of our world. Also, to the extent that OES achieves its goals, Terri and I will renew ourselves financially. We have mutually committed to donating a portion of the money we earn from OES to EPGW's revolving loan fund. In this way, we know we can fulfill our larger commitment to confront economic and social poverty through entrepreneurship. To that end, we will never ever give up. So, stay tuned!

About the Author

Brian Cunningham has more than forty years of experience as an engineer, a venture-backed entrepreneur, and advisor to venture capital firms and their start-ups. He began his professional career in 1960 as a physicist at the Naval Ordnance Laboratory and at NASA Goddard, in Greenbelt, Maryland.

In 1965, he co-founded Electronic Sales Associates (ESA), an organization that specialized in high-speed computer printers, tape drives, mini-computers, and digital data acquisition systems. From 1969 to 1989, Mr. Cunningham served as the chairman and CEO of CES Corporation, an outgrowth of ESA.

In May 1994, the board of trustees of his alma mater, St. Francis University, awarded Mr. Cunningham an honorary doctorate in humanities for his contributions to the homeless and the working poor members of society.

Since 1991, Mr. Cunningham has served as the chief executive of Entrepreneurial Advocates, Inc., an organization he founded that is dedicated to the success and support of entrepreneurs. He is also the founder and CEO of the Entrepreneurial Partnership of Greater Washington (EPGW), a nonprofit organization that teaches a variety of entrepreneurship and self-esteem courses to financially challenged inner-city residents.

Mr. Cunningham is a father of nine and grandfather of twenty-two (as of 2004). He enjoys sailing, woodworking, and walking with his wife, Terri, and as many of the children and grandchildren who can tolerate his God-inspired energy.

This book provides an autobiographical description of my entrepreneurial journey, including the good, bad, ugly, and humorous steps along my twenty-year journey through a valley of desperate despair to the thrill of corporate victory. I'm very proud of and grateful for the performance of CES Corporation, the subject of this book, as it grew from a few founders who had an idea to a thousand highly motivated associates on four continents. We competed, head-to-head, with the best of the best, including IBM, NCR, and Burroughs, companies thousands of times our size. And we won almost 60 percent of the competitive encounters. After four years of start-up losses, we achieved sixteen years of consecutively increasing profitability, returning more than thirty times their initial investment to our founding investors. While I personally made 98 percent of the mistakes an entrepreneur could make, I persisted, learned, and survived. Finally, CES thrived. I hope you enjoy this book as much as I enjoyed the journey.

Brian Cunningham, January 14, 2007

Endnotes

---

[1] The Free Press. A Division of Macmillan Inc. 866 Third Ave NY, NY, 10022, ISBN 0-02-903610-0, 1987

[2] "Now I'll get back to my discussion with the Office of Advocacy, U.S. Small Business Administration. According to their latest figures, approximately one-half of all new businesses will survive for at least five years, which is of course not anywhere near the dismal statistics that some people would have you believe. After five years, the survival rate jumps considerably. The moral of this story is that if you're considering starting your own business, a 50/50 chance of survival isn't that bad-those odds certainly don't seem to deter people from getting married. They key thing to remember is to do your homework, learn from others and do everything you can to make sure that the business you decide to start is part of the 50 percent that do survive."
Article by Ron Flavin, December 28, 2007, *The Peoples*

[3] Personal observations of Brian Cunningham

[4] For entrepreneurial companies both the risks and the returns tend to be much greater. My observations included a paper presented at an SEC meeting by the venture capital firm, New Enterprise Associates (NEA) based on four thousand investment-grade business plans. At an SEC conference in the early 1990s, NEA, a successful and sophisticated venture capitalist, reported that out of four thousand investment plans submitted to the company, 300 merited further investigation. Of these three hundred, fifty were investment grade candidates requiring intense due diligence. Out of these 50 opportunities, NEA finally made twenty investments. After many years of nurturing and development, the results of these twenty investments fell into three broad categories:

- Six (30 percent) achieved expectations returning five to a hundred times on the investment.

- Eight (40 percent) were nonperformers (neither failed nor met expectations).

- Six (30 percent) were losers, in that they failed within three to five years.

Returning to the initial four thousand submissions, the above results mean that only 0.15 percent of the companies that submitted business plans and only 30 percent (six of the twenty) of those who passed sophisticated investor due diligence were actually able to produce results meeting their own and their investors' expectations. Beyond the experience of sophisticated professional investors like NEA, other data suggests that in the long run only 20 percent of all new businesses in the general population succeed.

[5] *Top Management Strategy*, by Benjamin M. Tregoe and John W. Zimmerman<Kepner-Tregoe, Princeton, New Jersey, 1980 & 1999

[6] *The Daily Drucker*, Harper Collins Publisher, 2004

[7] Kofi Annan, former United Nations secretary-general

978-0-595-43221-9
0-595-43221-2

Printed in the United States
203313BV00002B/1-78/P

9 780595 432219